From Hacienda to Bungalow

From Hacienda to Bungalow

Northern New Mexico Houses, 1850-1912

Agnesa Lufkin Reeve

Published in cooperation with the
Historical Society of New Mexico

UNIVERSITY OF NEW MEXICO PRESS
Albuquerque

Library of Congress Cataloging in Publication Data

Lufkin Reeve, Agnesa.
    From hacienda to bungalow: northern New Mexico houses 1850–
1912 / Agnesa Lufkin Reeve.—1st ed.
        p.   cm.
    "Published in cooperation with the Historical Society of New
Mexico."
    Bibliography: p.
    Includes index.
    ISBN 0-8263-1022-2.   ISBN 0-8263-1031-1 (pbk.)
    1. Architecture, Domestic—New Mexico. 2. Eclecticism in archi-
tecture—New Mexico. 3. Architecture, Spanish Colonial—New
Mexico. 4. Architecture, Modern—19th century—New Mexico.
5. Architecture, Modern—20th century—New Mexico. I. Title.
NA7235. N6L84 1988
728'.09789—dc19   87-18770

Contents

Foreword

The Historical Society of New Mexico is pleased to announce the publication of *From Hacienda to Bungalow*, the sixteenth volume in the historical series cosponsored with the University of New Mexico Press. The success of this partnership has enabled the publication of books that broaden the appreciation of the historical development of the Southwest.

In this handsomely produced volume, Agnes Lufkin Reeve explores the diverse architectural heritage of northeastern New Mexico. Her focus is the far-reaching social, cultural, and architectural change initiated by the penetration of the railroad into New Mexico Territory in 1880. Aside from the development of the Territorial Style, little architectural change had occurred since the United States occupied New Mexico in 1846. Transporting vast quantities and varieties of building materials, prefabricated elements, and eastern fashions to the territory, the railroad sparked an architectural revolution throughout the region. The dynamics of this abrupt visual change are the subject of Dr. Reeve's study.

Setting the stage for the decades following 1880, the first chapters describe the architecture of the region in the decades prior to the railroad era. When the Americans invaded the Southwest, they entered a world of unfamiliar architectural form and materials. Although they adopted some of them, they changed many more methods, materials, and motifs.

Dr. Reeve's work is an invaluable addition to the understanding of New Mexico's architectural development. Her study will be essential reading for the student of southwestern architecture.

The Board of Directors of the Historical Society of New Mexico is made up of interested citizens and representatives from the academic community. The current officers and members of the Board are: Spencer Wilson, president; Charles Bennett, first vice president; Michael L. Olsen, second vice president; John W. Grassham, secretary; M. M. Bloom, Jr., treasurer; and Carol Cellucci, executive director. The members of the Board are: John P. Conron, Thomas E. Chavez, Richard N. Ellis, Austin Hoover, John P. Wilson, Albert H. Schroeder, William J. Lock, Octavia Fellin, Myra Ellen Jenkins, Susan Berry, Darlis Miller, Morgan Nelson, Robert R. White , Robert J. Torrez, and Elvis E. Fleming.

Preface

As the tide of American trans-Mississippi expansion rolled westward in the eighteenth and early nineteenth centuries, it engulfed mountains and deserts and to the Southwest carried a flood of new ideas which, by the mid-nineteenth century, would inundate the two-hundred-year-old Spanish-Mexican society. One consequence which developed over seven or eight decades was that Anglo influences on domestic architecture in New Mexico left an imprint that is traceable in a series of specific structures and therefore affords material evidence of the wave of social change. Houses are accurate barometers of changing tastes; because they are the most personal and malleable architecture, they most quickly reflect their builders' developing tastes.

To focus closely on a limited number of structures, this study is confined to northeastern New Mexico: Raton on the north, Santa Fe on the south, Springer on the east and El Rito on the west (See Maps 1 and 2). The time frame encompasses mention of several, and detailed examination of two, structures from the mid-nineteenth century that represent, respectively, the state of New Mexican architecture at the time of the first large-scale Anglo intrusion, and the installation that embodied that intrusion.[1] A watershed year politically, 1912 serves as a reasonable date to mark the end of an unrelieved movement away from traditional New Mexican architecture.

For several reasons the majority of examples used in the book are houses which were still standing when researched. First, there is a nebulous but substantial understanding that comes only on direct confrontation with what historian Brooke Hindle calls a "three-dimensional embodiment" of history.[2] In trying to explain the value of material objects to the study of history, Hindle says "somehow many objects belong to the viewer and are firmly a part of his understanding of history in a way that would have been totally impossible had he never seen them."[3] Second, the houses that have survived a century or longer are more apt to have been built as fine homes; therefore, perhaps they have been better cared for. Sometimes, at least, they have been less altered. It is true that an elegant house that stands a hundred years cannot be called *typical* because not a great many others are like it. On the other hand, these are precisely the houses to illustrate the evolution of architectural styles because they were built by influential men—ranchers, merchants, politicians and others—of both Anglo and Hispanic descent who were familiar with new trends and followed them. Historian Ivor Noel Hume makes a further point in favor of the *non-typical*. "If, in our quest for the group norm, we lose sight of the individual and the anomalies that make him so, we are in danger of rejecting archaeology's greatest potential, to wit: the opportunity to reach out to the individuals who made the American colonial experience."[4] Third, when a house exists at the time of study, detail is available to the student in a measure far beyond that contained in written reports.

Historic photographs, an invaluable resource both for structures now demolished and for those that have sustained remodeling and "restoration," are included here whenever possible. Also incorporated are a number of drawings made by the Historic American Buildings Survey, including floor plans and elevations. The latter reveal architectural mass and line sometimes more clearly than is possible in photographs.

Several types of material are helpful in analyzing the houses and their significance as social evidence. By comparing details and plans of many New Mexican houses with those shown in U.S. publications such as pattern books and *American Architect and Building News*, it is apparent that a local builder's ambition often was to emulate a typical "American" house.

Helping him in this ambition were not only the late nineteenth-century professional publications but also mail-order catalogs, specifically those of Sears, Roebuck, and Montgomery Ward. These made available nationally distributed and mass-produced products such as screen doors. In addition to copying or buying these elements, New Mexican artisans and homeowners could take advantage of published articles that praised or deplored one style or another, and which gave complete descriptions of furnishings and interior decor as well as exteriors.

The changing perceptions of *home* are as valid indices of evolution as the houses themselves. The most significant material testifying to perceptions of domestic establishments comes from accounts written by travelers through early New Mexico, such as Susan Magoffin and William Bell, newspapers of the day, and such other critics and commentators who had occasion to discuss New Mexico and domestic architecture of the United States in general.

Also valuable for gaining some understanding of the social metamorphosis that took place as Anglo ideas gained dominance in the Territory are the works of those writers who have imaginatively explored the phenomenon and given substance to their fiction by meticulous historical research. Volumes such as *The Conquest of Don Pedro* by Harvey Fergusson, *Centuries of Santa Fe* by Oliver La Farge, and *A Distant Trumpet* by Paul Horgan, weave social history into their tales and add texture to the warp and weft of history.

Without pretending to exhaust the subject, this exploration of changing design in domestic architecture helps illuminate the impact of the Anglo invasion of New Mexico. By 1912, as her domestic architecture demonstrates, New Mexico had, over a period of three decades, moved from the social climate of a backwater of the Spanish Empire and the Mexican Republic, with an accompanying resistance to change, into the conglomerate and fast evolving pattern of North American life.

Among the many people who contributed greatly to this study are those from the University of New Mexico who inspired with their knowledge and enthusiasm. The first was Bainbridge Bunting, whose unquenchable verve made architectural history engrossing; Charles Biebel, Ferenc Szasz, and Douglas George brought that same vitality to social and art history. In Santa Fe, John Conron was of incalculable help both as architect and editor, and Myra Ellen Jenkins the most lively and omniscient of historians. Gay Gerhardt Law, who crisscrossed northern New Mexico with me, made fieldwork even more rewarding than usual. To my husband Jack, who provided encouragement, astute comment, and infinite patience, I am profoundly grateful. Finally, of course, I am indebted to those gracious New Mexicans who invited me to visit and photograph their homes, and to everyone who told me fascinating stories of the structures and their inhabitants.

From Hacienda to Bungalow

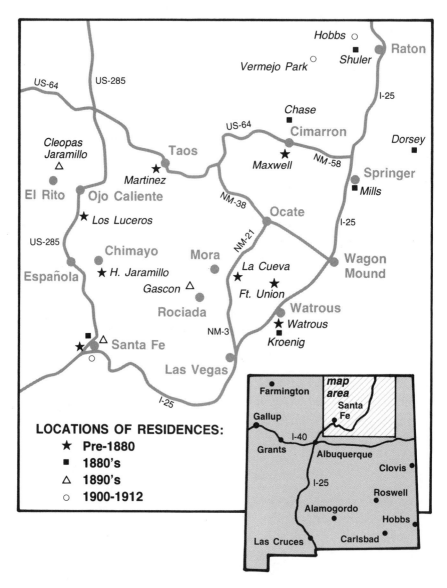

MAP . New Mexico. Research area is indicated on inset.
Houses discussed in text may be located by key.

1

Introduction

Architecture, the art of constructing buildings, is both older and newer in New Mexico than in most of the United States. It is older in that stone and adobe buildings were raised, sometimes in multiple stories, as early as A.D. 700, centuries before any permanent structures appeared east of the Mississippi. Not many ancient structures have survived, but still extant at Taos Pueblo are portions of buildings the conquistador Coronado found occupied in 1540, sixty-seven years before Jamestown was founded—eighty years before the Pilgrims landed at Plymouth.[1]

On the other hand, architecture is newer to the region because New Mexico was so remote from Spanish cities to the south and Anglo cities to the north that it was not until the nineteenth century that it was exposed to new ideas or sophisticated refinements. During the seventeenth and eighteenth centuries—a period when the American colonists were building more and more lavishly—the homes of this mountain and desert region remained unchanged. In the 1750s, for example, when the British colonies saw the creation of such elegant residences as Gunstan Hall and Carter's Grove in Virginia and Longfellow House in Massachusetts, the New Mexican house was still a simple adobe box.

Not only were communication and inspiration meager, but resources were too. Far from having fulfilled the Spaniards' dreams of cities paved in gold, New Mexico barely yielded a living for her struggling inhabitants. If they had conceived of palatial homes few could have afforded them. Even the missions of New Mexico lacked elaborate embellishments later found in those of California or Texas, partly because of the long overland haul, but also because there simply was no money.

There was, however, land. It was the policy of the Spanish and later the Mexican government to make grants of land to encourage colonization even though, especially during the Spanish reign, an enormous distance, and hence time, separated the far frontier from the makers and administrators of laws. Nevertheless, the Spanish Recopilación de las Indias provided that "lands shall be distributed with excess among discoverers, and old settlers, and their descendants, who are to remain in the country and those best qualified shall be preferred . . ."[2] So it was not difficult for a colonist to get title to his own place; he simply petitioned the crown for a vacant piece of land suitable for a farm or ranch. Most of the grants were in the north central part of the Territory and along the Rio Grande, since the availability of water was essential to a settler in this arid country.

For more than two hundred years after the settlement of Santa Fe in 1610, the residents of northeastern New Mexico Territory continued as their forebears had begun, farming and fending off, sometimes successfully, the depredations of marauding Indians. Although primarily agricultural, the region had a military and administrative center in Santa Fe, and it supported intermittent trade over the trail to Chihuahua, Mexico. The population outside Santa Fe was scattered along the Río Grande, sometimes with a few houses clustered in hamlets and often single families living on their own land. Throughout the eighteenth century these isolated groups were vulnerable to Indian attack, but resisted attempts by the government in Santa Fe to force them to consolidate into defensible villages.[3] Records indicate most families irrigated sufficient land to cultivate their own beans, chili, maize, and other vegetables, along with raising livestock, usually sheep. Historian Jessie Bailey has discussed a Spanish survey made in 1695 near the village of Chimayo which describes the neighborhood of small landholders, including buildings which were occupied before the Indian revolt of 1680.

[There was an] hacienda that once belonged to Miguel Lujan. There the houses were still standing and in them lived the owner with his family. He cultivated and irrigated only sufficient land for one family and raised a suitable number of cattle. This hacienda bordered upon that of Marcos de Herrera, whose family claimed also another hacienda below . . . beyond that was a hacienda belonging to Juan Griego, the most desirable then viewed because of its capacity to house two families and its abundant pasturage . . . The hacienda of Pedro de la Cruz was visited, which boasted a one-room abode and only enough land for one colonist and his family.[4]

A family living on one of these holdings was almost self-sufficient. For the most part, food was raised on the place, furniture and clothing was simple and handmade, and all were sheltered in a house which was also simple and handmade. Unlike many of its seventeenth and eighteenth century counterparts in the Atlantic seaboard colonies, the New Mexican house did not have gables and glazed windows, and its furnishings seldom included mahogany sideboards and oriental rugs. The setting contributed to these architectural and decorative differences. To the north the American frontier moved westward, leaving peace and comfort to develop in its wake. New Mexico remained a frontier.[5]

This difference in the scale of luxury and comfort between East and West contributed to the unfavorable comparisons made by Yankees after the Santa Fe Trail was opened in 1821, and was largely responsible for the scorn with which things New Mexican were regarded by the visitors. This attitude, of course, reinforced Anglos in their determination to reshape the Southwest in their own image.

Most Anglos who entered New Mexico before the Mexican Revolution and most of those who followed later over the Santa Fe Trail were not favorably impressed by anything New Mexican, and certainly not by the local architecture. Lieutenant Zebulon Pike, entering Santa Fe in 1806, thought the town had the appearance of a "fleet of the flat-bottomed boats" which descended the Ohio River.[6] About fifty years later, an observant traveler remarked that the city had "more the appearance of a colony of brick-kilns than a collection of human habitation" (Fig. 1).[7]

1. Santa Fe in 1846, from J. W. Abert's *Western America in 1846–47* (San Francisco, 1966). Flags can be seen flying from the Governor's Palace in the center of the city, and from Fort Marcy on the hill to the right. This view left visitors unimpressed with New Mexican architecture.

For the next three decades there was little change in the architectural scene. There was primarily one material used in domestic construction, adobe, with three style variations: Indian, Spanish Colonial and Territorial. These three types were made of adobes (or sometimes in the case of structures in the river valley locations, of *terrones*), although owners built with stone where it was available along the eastern fringe of the Rockies. In addition, the highland areas saw log construction, both vertical, *jacal*, and horizontal, but the common New Mexican house was a collection of adobe boxes, the width of the boxes determined by the length of the beams, *vigas*, used for roof

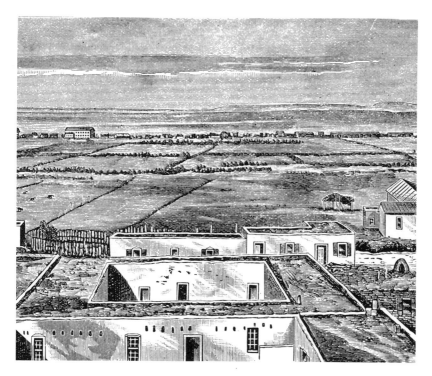

2. Las Vegas in 1880. H. T. Wilson's sketch shows adobe houses arranged around placitas in foreground, in Old Las Vegas. Houses of New Las Vegas, in background, display "American" style. From Andrew Gregg, *New Mexico in the Nineteenth Century* (Albuquerque, 1968).

support.[8] In view of the common material, architectural historian Bainbridge Bunting points out that the primary difference among Indian, Spanish and Anglo communities was the arrangement of the cube-shaped units. "The Indians tended to pile their cubes into irregular pyramids, like a pile of sugar lumps . . . the Spaniards arranged their cubes in a single file to form a series of rooms . . . the Americans . . . dispersed individual living units through the countryside."[9] H. T. Wilson's 1880 drawing of Las Vegas shows linearly arranged Spanish houses in the foreground, the files of rooms forming an **L** or square (Fig. 2.).

The adobe house in 1880 was essentially the same as it had been in 1780 and even in 1680. The basic unit used was the adobe, sun-dried brick made of straw mixed with mud and poured in forms. These were stacked to form the walls, cemented together with adobe mortar. Two coats of adobe plaster finished the walls. The roof was also of mud, its supporting structure consisting of the round vigas, crossed by a layer of small poles, *latias,* or split logs. The simplest early New Mexican house was one room deep, often set into a south-facing hillside for protection against the weather, or at least turning its back on the elements that beset it from the north and west. The depth of the room was determined by the length of available vigas, usually about fifteen feet—any unused length was allowed to project outside the wall. When more space was needed, a room could be extended in length. An open porch, *portal,* provided communication between rooms, though there might also be interior openings. Occasionally large houses were built around a patio, *placita,* with a portal affording both a passageway and an outdoor living space.

The recently appointed United States Attorney in New Mexico in 1856, W. W. H. Davis, described the adobe house as he encountered it in Santa Fe, and further pointed out that the town had the regularity of "all Spanish-built towns," the main streets extending in a gridiron from the corners of a central plaza.[10]

To the native Indian method of using puddled adobe, the Spaniards contributed the practice of molding mud into bricks. Their better tools of iron enabled them to employ vigas of larger dimension, thereby increasing the width of rooms from the Indians' six to fourteen feet up to fifteen feet.[11] The Spaniards also built rooms longer than the Indians', preferring one multiple-use space to many small ones.[12] Susan Magoffin, writing in 1846, describes her house's four rooms, the fourth one of which was

> the reception room, parlour, dining room, and in short room of all work. This is a long room with dirt floor (as they all have) plank ceiling, and nicely white-washed sides. Around one half to the height of six feet is tacked what may be called a schreen [sic] for it protects ones back from the white wash, if he should

chance to lean against it: it is made of calico, bound at each edge, and looks quite fixy; the seats, which are mostly cushioned benches, are placed against it—the floor too at the same end of the room is covered with a kind of Mexican carpeting; made of wool and coloured black and white only. In short we may consider this great hall as two rooms, for one half of it is carpeted and furnished for the parlour, while the other half has a naked floor, the dining table and all things attached to that establishment to occupy it.[13]

Davis also describes this sort of room and provides additional details.[14]

The ceiling is never plastered, but in those of the wealthier classes the beams that support the roof are planed and painted in various colors, and sometimes an artificial ceiling is made by tacking bleached muslin to them . . . In some sections of the country, small round sticks are laid from beam to beam in herringbone style and painted red, blue, or green; but it is only a choice room that is ornamented in this manner. The fire-place is built in one corner of the room, and occupies a small space. The mouth is somewhat in the shape of a horse-shoe, not generally more than eighteen inches or two feet in height, and the same in width at the bottom. The back is slightly concave instead of being a plane surface, and the little circular hearth in front is raised a few inches above the level of the floor. The use of andirons is unknown, the wood being placed on end against the back of the fireplace.[15]

In contrast, a Taos Indian family's home in the pueblo, for example, might well have been one room of a many-roomed building, that room no more than twelve feet by fifteen feet and scantily furnished with a few homemade clay pots and dressed skins. In the 1881 sketch of a Taos Pueblo interior, the absence of furniture is obvious; the main article visible is the adobe bench, *banco*, built in the wall on the left (Fig. 3). The roof construction is apparent, with vigas supporting poles of pine or aspen, latias, which in turn support the mud roof. The window opening is filled only with bars of wood between wooden lintel and sill. The low door has a high sill; an intruder is at a disadvantage if he has to stoop to enter. Either the room is on

3. Interior of Taos Pueblo, 1881. Except for the ladder and roof entrance, this room differs little structurally from a Spanish Colonial interior. The latter would have added to the furnishings a simple chair and table and, perhaps, a chest. Drawing from Andrew Gregg, *New Mexico in the Nineteenth Century* (Albuquerque, 1968).

an upper level or the window and door are recent additions, as the ground floor was without openings originally, entered only through the hole in the roof.

The Taos Pueblo of the eighteenth century was impressive in overall size if not in individual rooms, and in the twentieth century it looks very much the same except for doors and windows which were created later. Most Spanish colonial houses, on the other hand, have disappeared or been radically altered, only a few examples surviving with enough integrity to give a general appearance of the mode. The Severino Martínez house in Taos represents a New Mexican hacienda, modest in

4. Sena House and placita, Santa Fe. The second-story ballroom of this nineteenth-century house, reached by the outside stairway visible in the photograph, served as a temporary meeting place for the legislative assembly after the territorial capitol burned in 1892. Photograph, 1980.

comparison to the haciendas of northern Mexico, but consisting of a sizeable residence supported by various outbuildings, corrals, etc. El Zaguán, the Juan José Prada, and Sena houses in Santa Fe are differing versions of urban residences of the period (Fig. 4).

Not all early New Mexican homes were limited to the bare necessities. Both Magoffin and Davis visited in homes of the wealthy, the *ricos*, the former more sympathetically. In describing the *sala* of Don Mariano Chávez in 1846, Mrs. Magoffin says it is "well furnished with handsome Brussels carpet, crimson worsted curtains, with gilded rings and cornice, white marble slab pier tables—hair and crimson worsted chairs,

5. Father Gallegos's house in Albuquerque. Abert's 1846 sketch shows calico covering the lower half of the wall with pictures and mirrors hanging above. The ceiling appears to be supported by squared beams rather than vigas. J. W. Abert, *Western America in 1846–47* (San Francisco, 1966).

chandelabras . . . eight or ten gilt-framed mirrors all around the wall."[16]

Davis also commented on gilt-framed mirrors, but less happily. According to his account, the sala of General Manuel Armijo

> exhibited a singular mixture of modern elegance and barbaric taste. In one corner stood an elegant canopied brass bedstead, after the most approved Parisian style, while in close contact was another clumsily made of pine and painted a dirty red; heavy wooden benches seemed misplaced beside velvet-covered

chairs and a beautiful Turkey carpet; and the time-stained wooden beams that supported the roof were reflected in twenty gilded mirrors that hung around the room.[17]

Time effects a shift in attitude, for in the latter half of the twentieth century this combination of rustic and sophisticated might be considered elegantly eclectic (Fig. 5).

Visiting another hacienda, Davis found the second-story room allotted him to be plain, furnished with a single bed, mattresses rolled up along the wall for seats, a rough pine table and a dirt floor (the dirt roof of the first floor), although his host, Don Tomás Cabeza de Baca, lived "surrounded with a throng of peones somewhat after the manner of the feudal lords of the Middle Ages."[18]

A type of building that was partially residential and wholly vital to the development of the Territory was the trading post. Some were large and famous throughout the region, such as Bent's Fort, built in 1833 on the north bank of the Arkansas River, the boundary between New Mexico and the United States (in present Colorado). Like most others, Bent's Fort served as a retail store and trading post, as well as a sort of rest and recreation oasis in the wilderness. According to Susan Magoffin, who stopped there, it also was exactly her "idea of an ancient castle."[19] The high, thick walls were built of adobe and some twenty-five rooms were built against them. One of these rooms was assigned to the Magoffins.

> It has a dirt floor, which I keep sprinkling constantly during the day; we have two windows, one looking out on the plain the other is on the patio or yard. We have our own furniture, such as bed, chairs, wash basin, table furniture, and we eat in our own room . . . They have one large room as a parlor; there are no chairs but a cushion next to the wall on two sides, so the company sit all around in a circle. There is no other furniture than a table on which stands a bucket of water, free to all.[20]

Another well-known trading post was Barclay's Fort, situated on the Sapello River near the town of La Junta de los Rios (now Watrous). Established about 1850, the business and property were put up for sale in 1853. The assets listed in the newspaper announcement show the scope of the operation.

Will be sold to the highest bidder . . . the place well known as Barclay's Fort, at Juncta de los Rios, including all the right, title interest in the surrounding Grant of five leagues, with out house corrals, etc., and ice house filled; a highly cultivated garden, with hot-bed frames and young fruit trees—and two hundred acres of land under cultivation, irrigated by two large acequias which also run a small mill capable of grinding thirty fanegas of grain per diem. Also a number of wagons, cattle, cows and calves, horses and hogs, with farming utensils of all kinds; a complete set of blacksmith's tools. Together with a general assortment of dry goods and groceries and a number of articles too numerous to mention here.[21]

Three years later Davis's visit to Barclay's Fort inspired him with a somewhat gloomy romanticism.

It is a large establishment, and, like the immense caravansaries of the East, serves as an abode for men and animals. From the outside it presents a rather formidable as well as neat appearance, being pierced with loop holes and ornamented with battlements. The rooms within were damp and uncomfortable and all the surroundings looked so gloomy, the hour being twilight, that it reminded me of some old state prison, where the good and the great of former times have languished away their lives.[22]

Some trading posts were cosier, being a part of the merchant's own house. Samuel Watrous had such an arrangement, also at La Junta, and Hermanegildo Martínez y Jaramillo added a "store" room to his Chimayo home (Fig. 6). John Bouquet, a Frenchman who in 1869 began reassembling the old Pojoaque estate of Nicolás Ortiz, built a complex that included his own home, a stagecoach station, a general store and a hostelry. At all the posts, information and ideas, as well as goods, were stock in trade.

From 1821 to about 1846, the year New Mexico came under United States control, these trading posts were witness to a period of slow change as a trickle of men, material, and ideas came over the Trail. In architecture, there appeared rough, simple hints of the Greek Revival Style which, although reaching a peak of popularity in the States about 1835, appeared only

6. Hermanegildo Jaramillo House in Chimayó, mid-nineteenth century. The store room projects at right. The entrance was at the end, now a triple window. Photograph, 1980.

minimally in New Mexico until after the Civil War, when trade greatly increased.

New Mexicans adorned their adobe boxes with a few simple wood trimmings, creating a style designated by Bunting as Early Territorial. After 1846, many more Yankees arrived to settle and build residences. These included large contingents of the United States Army, which had a strong impact on the building trades by introducing a much greater supply of manufactured goods, skilled workmen, and a more sophisticated version of the Greek Revival style.

The local adaptation of Greek Revival, Territorial, is charac-

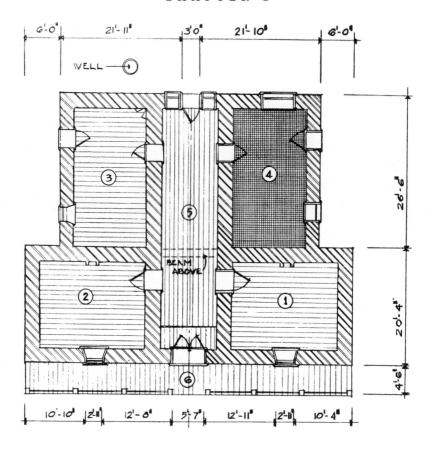

terized by a central hall plan with rooms ranged symmetrically on either side, and pedimented lintels over window and door
openings (Fig. 7). The pediments might be simple flat triangles, or be built up with moldings. Emphasis on the entrance
with overdoor and side lights, and a brick coping on the parapet of a flat roof, are often additional features. Both the symmetrical plan and the pediment detail, along with white accents,
proclaim the debt to Greek Revival.

The construction of permanent United States Army bases
in the Territory was in large part responsible for the acceptance
of the new architectural appearance. Fort Union, established

8. Officers' Row at Fort Union, c. 1885. The crisp lines and fresh white trim of the Territorial style as illustrated at the fort had an important influence on the architectural tastes of the area. Museum of New Mexico.

7. (*Facing page*) Plan of the Leandro Martínez House, Taos, 1862. The plan displays the characteristics of the Territorial idiom with rooms arranged symmetrically on either side of a central hall. From Bainbridge Bunting, *Early Architecture in New Mexico* (Albuquerque, 1976).

in 1851 to protect communities and travelers on the Santa Fe Trail from marauding Indians, operated from hastily and poorly built log cabins until 1863. In the years from 1863 to 1869, however, a handsome garrison rose, replacing the silhouette of crumbling log cabins with the crisp lines of Territorial. The precise symmetry of the style was particularly suitable as a symbol of an orderly military operation. Understandably, the fresh look of the fort inspired civilian building taste, and spread the popularity of the wide hall and white pedimented lintel (Fig. 8).

New sawmills, more competent carpenters and a wider range of tools and materials arriving over the Trail enabled citizens to indulge in innovations. Houses throughout the Territory began to display Greek Revival detail. Fort Marcy in Santa Fe, extensively remodeled and rebuilt in the early 1870s, using the same architectural idiom, reinforced the trend. Some mid-nineteenth century residences still in use in Santa Fe have the coping and pediments which were in vogue when they were built or remodeled: including the Borrego, Gregorio Crespin and Pinckney R. Tully Houses.

Soon after the middle of the nineteenth century, there began to appear examples of the two-story, veranda-embellished mansion of the ricos, many with Territorial trim and many whose second story and double portal were later additions. One of the latter is La Cueva, built in the Mora Valley in the 1850s and '60s by Vicente Romero, a rancher who controlled 33,000 acres. Las Vegas merchant José Albino Baca demonstrated his wealth in an 1850s three-story adobe which was, by all accounts, impressively elaborate. The interior boasted a walnut staircase and a ballroom on the third floor. The exterior featured a two-story portal with regiments of square posts and segmental arches. It has been called "the New Mexican equivalent of an elaborate American Greek Revival veranda."[23] Los Luceros in Rio Arriba County and Phoenix Ranch at Watrous are further examples of this western version of the Greek Revival mansion.

By 1873 changes were appearing in both new and old residences, to the extent that the *Santa Fe New Mexican* commented on the larger windows and doors, and the fact that windows opened onto the street front, not just into the placita.[24] After the railroad entered the Territory in 1879, an enormous influx of both Anglo materials and Anglo ideas soon rode the rails into New Mexico. Included in this onslaught were Eastern architectural styles, both those new in the States and those already old-fashioned there, but all fresh to New Mexicans. In the decade following the arrival of the railroad, American ideas were received enthusiastically and indiscriminately, and domestic architecture reflected this acceptance. Almost every new house, although still built of adobe, displayed at least some detail imported from the States, whether it be from the then fashionable Queen Anne style, or the twenty years out-of-date (in the East) Italianate style.

In the Territory the forms were usually applied superficially, a Queen Anne porch or a mansard roof incorporated into a traditional adobe structure, so that the finished product was not Queen Anne nor Mansard, nor even Midwest Farmhouse, but a new hybrid unique to this part of the Southwest. Efforts of ambitious homeowners, both long time residents and those newly arrived, were directed toward making the domestic architecture of the Territory duplicate that of Ohio, Kansas, or any other area of the U.S. which had access to building material catalogs and architectural pattern books. Using these materials and models in conjunction with older Spanish–Pueblo methods of construction, builders created a style with a character of its own, a solid mass of earth-color adobe iced with decorative wood trim.

Because the adobe house has always expressed a heavy sculptured mass rather than space enclosed by a skin of mud-plaster, the addition of thin, precise, and airy wood scrolls, brackets, and posts produces an effect of incongruity, eternally startling, as surprising in the hundredth example as in the first. The disparity is greatly relieved, however, when another visual force of sufficient size is introduced, that is, an element expressing a density somewhere between solid adobe and lacy fretwork. The example of this ameliorating influence most often seen is the two-story portal, which not only serves to link interior and exterior spaces, but also projects a control of volume sufficiently powerful to be easily conceived as a natural adjunct of the primary mass.

A rather appealing house in Galisteo (c. 1890) illustrates this inconsistency at its most apparent (Fig. 9). The perfectly plain adobe box has attached to its facade what almost could be a segment of a Victorian gazebo. Inspiration for the design could have come from a number of pattern books available. For example, in Cummings and Miller's *Victorian Architectural Details* of 1868, Plate 48 shows various designs for fences cut out of "inch stuff," with Figure 3 bearing some resemblance to the Galisteo balustrade (Fig. 10).[25]

The Melvin W. Mills mansion in Springer (1880) dilutes the impact of a very large adobe block with a mansard roof as well as the two-story portal. With the upper edge of the block soft-

9. House in Galisteo, c. 1890. The house presents a block of adobe pierced by windows at regular intervals and individualized with a porch boasting columns, balustrade, spindle frieze, and cut-out brackets. Photograph, 1981.

10. Marcus Fayette Cummings and Charles Crosby Miller's pattern book published in 1868 shows designs similar to those on the Galisteo house. *Victorian Architectural Details* (N.Y., 1978).

ened by the sloping mansard, the portal encircling three sides allows the house to relate to its site comfortably, reflecting the rise of the land and surrounding trees. This trend continued through the 1890s, with builders adding Eastern detail, disguising adobe to make it appear more Eastern, or building houses that were Eastern or Midwestern in every way except wall material which continued to be, in general, adobe.

By 1900 the classic New Mexican adobe was rarely constructed, and even the use of adobe for houses of other styles lost popularity. The Territory was wealthier and its well-to-do residents and visitors disdained things New Mexican as backward

and undesirable. Ironically, this almost complete triumph of Eastern models which coincided with New Mexico's statehood would be followed with a revival of interest in the Spanish–Pueblo adobe house.

In order to demonstrate the impact of an enormous number of new ideas, patterns, and manufactured items on home design, and to chart the variations on new architectural themes and their relation to new social themes, it is necessary to look further, and in more detail, at the state of domestic architecture before those new elements were available and those new themes heard.

2

Two Haciendas
and a Trading Post,
1820s–1850s

In order to paint an accurate picture of domestic architecture in New Mexico before the arrival of influences from the North, it is not enough to describe only the modest home of the average family. Although the majority of homes were small, it would present a distorted image to suggest there were not notable exceptions. The exceptions contain the seeds of change because these houses represent the endeavor and attitudes of some of the region's most prominent and forward-looking people.

Because practical considerations of site and material virtually eliminated any chance for variation, domestic architecture of the Spanish colonial period in New Mexico was homogenous. With a few regional exceptions, walls were of adobe, plastered with mud; flat roofs were of mud supported on vigas and latias; floors were packed earth.[1] Iron was scarce and expensive, so doors were hung using pintels, extensions of the stile on one side shaped to fit into sockets in lintel and sill, allowing the door to swing. Windows were small and usually fitted with wooden bars and shutters, although sometimes an opening might be covered with translucent selenite.[2]

The linear system of Spanish Colonial building lent itself to several arrangements: a straight line of rooms, an **L** shape, a **U** shape, or a square enclosing a placita. All of these plans were used in both urban and rural homes, though not many fami-

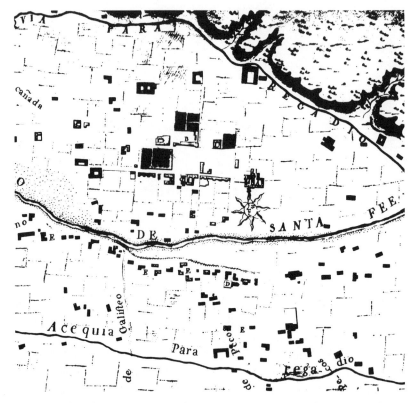

11. Joseph de Urrutia Map of Santa Fe, 1766–68. The various house configurations, square, **L**-shaped, **U**-shaped, and a single line, are all clearly defined. Copy in Museum of New Mexico.

lies were affluent enough to build a complete square. The various shapes are clearly visible in early maps such as the 1766–68 map of Santa Fe by Joseph de Urrutia (Fig. 11). Sometimes a house was first built with a single file of two or three rooms, then subsequent rows of rooms added at right angles, eventually completing the square. During the years when the threat of Indian attacks had to be considered, large rural ranch headquarters, *haciendas*, were usually planned not only with living rooms arranged in a protective square, but with shelter for livestock and storage located in an adjoining rectangle (Fig. 12).

Although much remodeled, the Antonio Severino Martínez

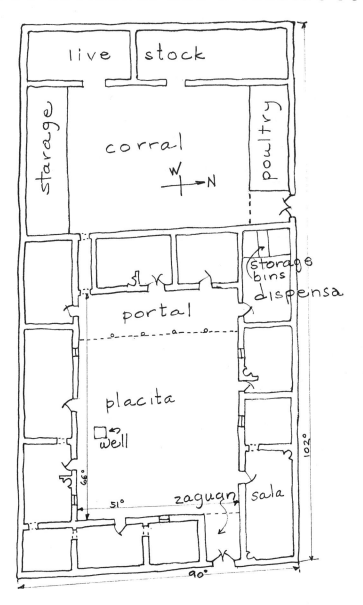

12. Hacienda plan. In this hypothetical plan drawn by Bainbridge Bunting, the placita-centered house is adjoined by a protected corral and storage area. *Early Architecture in New Mexico* (Albuquerque, 1976).

13. Severino Martínez Hacienda, Taos. This house is a re-creation of the 1820s building. Its size, block shape, and windowless walls emphasize the fortress-like quality. Photograph, 1980.

14. Martínez Hacienda, Taos. The mud-plastered adobe walls, hollowed log canales, and corner buttress are characteristic of Spanish colonial structures. Photograph, 1980.

15. Plan of Martínez Hacienda. Rooms 10–14 at lower left probably comprised the original house. The zaguán is space 15. The *sala mayor* may have been comprised of Rooms 5 and 6, at the end of the placita. *Taos Adobes* (Santa Fe, 1964)

hacienda near Taos, completed by 1827, serves to illustrate the simplicity and fortress-like quality of a rural Spanish colonial dwelling built by a wealthy and powerful family (Figs. 13, 14). It was designed with no exterior windows—only onto the placita—and with a parapet which afforded protection for house-holders defending against Indian attackers.[3]

Most of the house was built between 1824 and 1827, but the four small rooms on the southeast corner (10, 11, 13, 14) were already old in 1824 when Don Severino bought the property (Fig. 15).[4] These rooms have lower floor levels and ceiling heights than later rooms, and are slightly narrower. As the plan

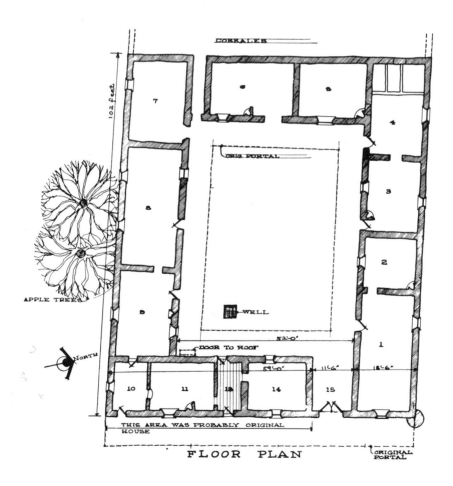

CORRALES

7

6

5

4

102 feet

ORIG. PORTAL

8

3

2

WELL

APPLE TREES

9

NORTH

DOOR TO ROOF

52'-0"

1

59'-0"

11'-6"

18'-6"

10

11

12

14

15

THIS AREA WAS PROBABLY ORIGINAL
HOUSE

ORIGINAL
PORTAL

FLOOR PLAN

shows, the house was then enlarged until it contained twelve rooms enclosing a placita. In one corner of the placita a narrow passage gives access to the rear of the house. Evidence indicates there existed a walled area providing protected corrals and storerooms adjacent to the main structure in the manner suggested by Bunting's hypothetical plan (See Fig. 12).

The house is quite large, 90 x 102 feet, its placita measuring 51 x 65 feet. Originally the entrance to the placita was through the eleven-foot-wide covered gate, *zaguán*, large enough for a horse drawn cart, and the only exterior opening. Not only is the entire house large, but it boasts several rooms of unusual size. The thirty-four-foot long Room One is called the "room of Doña Maria," and may be presumed to be the room left, along with Room Two, to the widow in the will of Don Severino.[5]

> Also, at the large house on the plaza of San Francisco del Ranchito there was given to her the room with the plank roof, and the little room with a plank roof, which together with thirteen and one-half varas at a peso and six reales the vara, with two doors, two windows, little room with a basement and with a small portal and picket fence "varandal" seven varas at one peso the vara, and the door of the basement with also the small portal of the room and four varas of that of the hall "sala" at four reales the vara.[6]

As the will makes clear, it was common practice to leave portions of a house to various members of a family. Predictably, this resulted in some structures being sound in one segment and decaying in another after a few years of disparate care.

> One of Don Severino's sons, José Maria de Jesús, received for a house the large hall *'sala mayor'* at the main residence at Ranchito de San Francisco, sixteen varas at a peso and six reales each for having a planked floor [sic], the double doors 'puerta de dos manos' at the same house at two pesos, the window at one: the storeroom 'dispensa' which continues from the hall in the same line, ten varas, at twelve reales, its door and iron lock two pesos, and the portal belonging to the large hall, which measures nine varas . . .[7]

Evidence suggests that Rooms Five and Six composed this sala mayor. Bunting points out that if thrown together, the

16. West wall of Martínez placita in 1923. The double door in the center of the wall would have been near the center of Rooms 5 and 6 together. The door at right might have been a window or no opening at all originally, as it lacks a pediment and is small, while the other two openings are large and pedimented. *Taos Adobes* (Santa Fe, 1964).

rooms formed a forty-four foot long sala, with two fireplaces and a double door.[8] Additionally, the dividing adobe partition appears to have been built later than the rest of the house. Measurements and double doors correspond with references in the will and one of the two windows appearing in the plan may well date from a later remodeling (Fig. 16.)

The dispensa left to José Maria de Jesús seems to have been Room Four, as measurements correspond to those in the will and it "continues from the hall in the same line." The other possibility would be Room Seven, which Bunting feels was always a storeroom because of its high barred window, but it

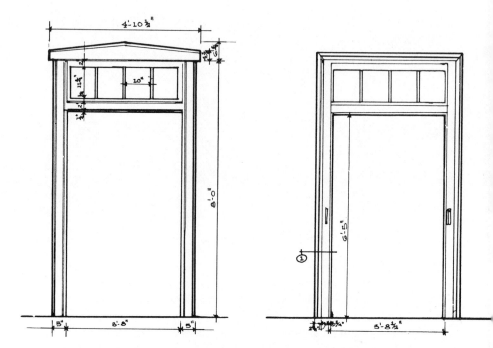

17. Details of the Martínez House. Exterior openings were capped with simple pediments, which interior facings lacked. In buildings which have been remodeled, the presence of a pediment on an inside door suggests a formerly exterior opening. *Taos Adobes* (Santa Fe, 1964).

is smaller than ten varas and is separated from the line of the sala by the passage to the rear.[9]

Of the individual rooms Don Severino bequeathed to members of his family, some had an accompanying portal, as in the "portal belonging to the large hall," but apparently the placita did not have portals on all sides until the 1860s.[10] The portals were simply constructed with round posts and no attempt to simulate capitals. Some window and door frames and shutters, however, are embellished with moldings and pediments, probably indicating a date later than 1827 (Fig. 17).

There would not have been a large number of establishments

as imposing as Don Severino's in any one area, as its size alone announced extraordinary wealth. It seems likely, therefore, that it served as a model for the Taos estate of the Coronel family in novelist Harvey Fergusson's *Grant of Kingdom*, set in the 1850s.

> The Coronel place stood on a low hill at the western edge of town, and was known therefore as La Loma. It looked almost as though it had been carved from the earth, or upthrust from it by some subterranean force—a great angular block of earthen wall, golden brown, plastered smooth, glinting in the sun with tiny bits of mica. Its windows were few, opaque with oiled paper and barred with wrought iron. A long narrow veranda ran across the front but no one ever sat there. The front entrance was a double door, iron-barred from within, which would have resisted a battering-ram. Behind the house was a square enclosed by adobe walls as high as the house itself, with cactus growing along its top. A solid double carriage gate, ten feet high, was the only way in from the rear. The house of Coronel was a very old house, a house of immense strength and stability, which kept its life secret and secluded, presented to the world a passive, impenetrable resistance.[11]

Although not faithful in every detail—there were no iron bars on the Martínez house—the author expresses the image of remote power so apparent in the structure (See Fig. 13). A "long, narrow veranda," that is, a portal, was added to the Martínez facade, but not until about the time of the Civil War (Fig. 18).[12]

As well as the exterior, the interior of the Martínez home appears to have been somewhat austere. Certainly it was much less elaborately furnished than the home of another New Mexican rico, Don Mariano Chávez, visited by Susan Magoffin in the 1840s, some twenty years after the date of Don Severino's will, and in which she found Brussels carpet and marble pier tables.[13]

In contrast, the list of household goods inherited by Don Severino's widow suggests domestic arrangements of simplicity: two large carpets, *alfombras*, and forty yards of woolen rug, *yerga*; four mattresses and pillows, six linen sheets, two day beds, *camapeses*, four stools, *taburetes*, two large tables, one cabinet, *almario*, two large boxes for clothes, *cajones de roperos*,

18. Martínez Facade in 1923. Portal has been added, and openings cut in addition to the original zaguán at right. *Taos Adobes* (Santa Fe, 1964).

and one grain box, *cajon areno*. She received as well a number of blankets and bolts of cloth.

Although his story was beginning in the 1850s, a quarter century after the Martínez will was written in 1827, Fergusson equipped the Coronel sala with equivalents of Doña Maria's effects, explaining that the house had not changed for three generations.

> The sala was a long room, running all the way across the front of the house, with a low heavy-raftered ceiling and walls washed white with gypsum. There were two fireplaces in opposite corners, both banked in this hot season with fragrant boughs of juniper. Some of the wealthy families now were beginning to buy furniture from St. Louis, but not the conservative Coronels. Their house remained as it had been for three generations. Along the walls were couches made by folding mattresses and covering them with great Navajo blankets in large patterns of black and red. A light red cotton cloth was hung against the lower part of the walls to keep the whitewash from rubbing off. There was no other furniture except a few homemade chairs with rawhide seats and two low tables of excellent workmanship.[14]

One item of luxury did appear among the Martínez effects. A large gilded mirror was left to the oldest son and most remembered member of the family, Padre Antonio José Martínez.[15] There being six children to share the estate with the widow, numbers of other boxes and rugs were accounted for, but the great wealth lay in land and livestock, not in goods meant for comfort or beauty.

With the exception of iron for a handful of locks, material for the Martínez hacienda came from the land on which it stood or the forests of nearby mountains. Lumber was felled, cut and hand dressed or used rough. The designs of both interior and exterior were determined by necessity and availability of building components. Wealth supplied good wool rugs and blankets, and a few silver vessels, but could add only size and iron locks to the kind of shelter which was built by the poorest peon.

THE MAXWELL HOUSE

By the middle of the nineteenth century a handful of Anglos had settled in northeastern New Mexico and there were a few large residences built by families not of Spanish descent. One of these was ranch headquarters for the Maxwell Ranch, located on the Cimarron River about fifty miles east of Taos and on the east side of the Sangre de Cristo mountain range. Lucien B. Maxwell, a mountain trapper and hunter, had married Luz Beaubien, daughter of Carlos Beaubien and heiress to half the enormous Miranda–Beaubien Land Grant. Through this connection and by purchase Maxwell acquired other interests in the Grant, and after years of maneuvering and litigation became owner of the entire Grant, the size of which ranged (in speculation and in fact) from 32,000 acres to 17,714,764 acres.[16] After marrying Luz Beaubien, Maxwell moved first in 1847 to Rayado, on the Grant, and then started building the town of Cimarron in the mid-1850s. It was in the center of what would become Cimarron that he built his mansion.

The mansion built in 1857–58 was a two-story adobe with walls four feet thick (Figs. 19, 20).[17] It has been described as resembling a French villa "with an open court inside and a verandah running the whole length of the building, covered by a projecting roof".[18] Colonel Henry Inman, a friend and visitor

19. Maxwell House, Cimarron, 1858. The two separate long gabled structures can be distinguished, with the veranda spanning the front. Date of the photograph is unknown, probably c. 1890–1900, Museum of New Mexico.

20. Maxwell House after the first fire. The rear section of the house (the women's wing) and part of the connecting wings can be seen. A second fire demolished this remaining structure. Photograph, early twentieth century, Museum of New Mexico.

of Maxwell's, calls the house "a palace when compared with the prevailing style of architecture in that country . . ." He goes on to describe its construction as "purely American," but in fact it was purely New Mexican, being of whitewashed adobe.[19] Inman fondly recalls his visits there.

> Some of its apartments were elaborately furnished, others devoid of everything except a table for card-playing and a game's complement of chairs. The principal room, an extended rectangular affair, which might properly have been termed the Baronial Hall, was almost bare except for a few chairs, a couple of tables, and an antiquated bureau. There Maxwell received his friends, transacted business with his vassals, and held high carnival at times.
>
> I have slept on its hardwood floor, rolled up in my blanket, with the mighty men of the Ute nation lying heads and points around me, as close as they could possibly crowd, after a day's fatiguing hunt in the mountains. I have sat there in the long winter evenings when the great room was lighted only by the cheerful blaze of the crackling logs roaring up the huge throats of its two fireplaces built diagonally across opposite corners, watching Maxwell, Kit Carson and half a dozen chiefs silently interchange ideas in the wonderful sign language . . . Frequently Maxwell and Carson would play the game of seven-up for hours.[20]

Life at Maxwell's owed a debt to the owner's past experiences as frontier trader and the friends he made in the West, but his house also owed something to his childhood in Illinois. One historian notes that "in many ways the general design of the house was reminiscent of styles prevalent at Kaskaskia when Lucien was growing up there, and in particular of his grandfather Menard's spacious residence overlooking the Mississippi" (Fig. 21).[21]

The residence was actually comprised of two houses separated by a high-walled patio. The rear structure contained the kitchen, storerooms, and a separate dining room for the ladies of the household and guests of that sex, according to the custom followed in Maxwell's day. In the men's dining room the table service of solid silver was laid daily for at least thirty—

friends and stage passengers. Colonel Inman writes with enthusiasm and explanation.

> Covers were laid daily for about thirty persons; for he had
> always many guests, invited or forced upon him in consequence
> of his proverbial munificence, or by the peculiar location of his
> manor-house which stood upon a magnificently shaded plateau
> at the foot of mighty mountains, a short distance from a ford on
> the Old Trail. As there were no bridges over the uncertain
> streams of the great overland route in those days, the ponderous
> Concord coaches, with their ever-full burden of passengers, were
> frequently water-bound, and Maxwell's the only asylum from
> the storm and flood; consequently he entertained many.[22]

The women not only ate separately, but were seldom seen
anywhere about the hacienda. "Only the quick rustle of a skirt,
or a hurried view of a reboso, as its wearer flashed for an instant
before some window or half-open door, told of their presence."[23]

The Maxwell's heavy Victorian furnishings had come over
the trail in wagons, and they gave character to each room.
"Room after room had its deep-piled carpets, heavy velvet draperies, gold-framed oil paintings . . . vast heavy dark tables in
the two dining rooms . . ."[24] Among the splendors of the mansion were four grand pianos, two upstairs and two downstairs,
and "the gaming rooms, one a billiard room, several smaller
ones fitted with green baize-covered tables for monte, poker,
chuck-a-luck and roulette."[25]

A Bostonian who visited Cimarron in 1881 found the mansion hard to believe.

> Our carriage drew up before a finely shaded lawn, some
> gentlemen stood on a broad veranda as we walked up the path,
> servants hastened out to take our luggage, a subdued, refined
> light glimmered from a hanging lamp through some lattice work
> beside the door—I rubbed my eyes; had I suddenly been
> transported to the Boston suburbs? A bric-a-brac, trophies of the
> hunt, Queen Anne decorations, portiers between whose rich
> folds were revealed rooms of palatial plan and style—then across
> a pretty turfed placita into a broad stair-case hall and we were
> shown into our cosey [sic], luxurious apartments. We seemed to
> have made some sort of Rip Van Winkle trip into the mountains,

21. The Pierre Menard House near Chester, Illinois, 1802. Maxwell's Grandfather Menard, a Quebec-born fur trader and a government official of the Illinois Territory, built this French colonial style house overlooking the Mississippi River. *A Pictorial History of Architecture in America* (New York, 1976).

but instead of alighting upon an uncanny crew, we had entered an enchanted castle.[26]

Cimarron as a town was not an enchanted land, however. In 1875, in the wake of a bitter race for representative to the Territorial legislature, the town exploded into anarchy, resulting in several murders, lynchings, and the rescue by the U.S. Cavalry of attorney (and newly elected delegate) Melvin W. Mills from the hands of a mob. The situation throughout 1875 was so bad that in January of 1876, Colfax County, including Cimarron, was attached to Taos County for judicial purposes (Fig. 22).

22. Cimarron in 1877. From the mesa east of town, looking southwest. The two-story stone flour mill is in the background, the Maxwell House, partly obscured by trees, in the center. Photograph, Museum of New Mexico.

Most of the strife in Cimarron and Colfax County—and it was strife so violent as to be dubbed "the Colfax County War" —was directly or indirectly attributable to Lucien Maxwell's Grant. Half of the almost two million acres finally alleged to be in the Grant was ardently held to have been public domain and legitimately homesteaded by small landholders (Fig. 23).[27]

Long after Maxwell's sale of his property in the late 1860s, and even after his death in 1875, "Grant" and "anti-Grant" were fighting words in Colfax County. Equally at issue in the Colfax struggle were attempts of various groups, especially the Santa Fe Ring, to control the Grant itself. Their machinations,

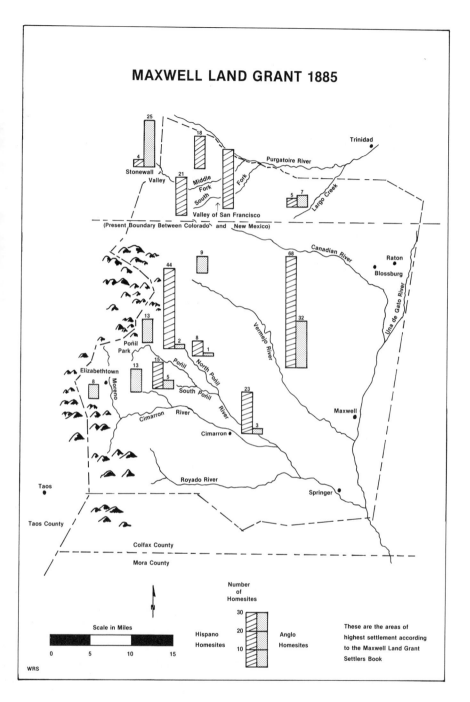

MAXWELL LAND GRANT 1885

Trinidad

25

18

4

Stonewall
Valley

21

Middle
Fork

South

Fork

Purgatoire River

Largo Creek

5 7

Valley of San Francisco

(Present Boundary Between Colorado and New Mexico)

Canadian River

Raton

Blossburg

9

44

68

32

Una de Gato River

13

Poñil
Park

Vermejo River

2

8

1

Elizabethtown

13

15

Poñil

North Poñil

8

5

Moreno

South Poñil

River

Maxwell

Cimarron   River

23

Taos

Cimarron

3

Taos County

Royado River

Springer

Colfax County

Mora County

N

Number
of
Homesites

Scale in Miles

30

20

Hispano
Homesites

Anglo
Homesites

These are the areas of
highest settlement according
to the Maxwell Land Grant
Settlers Book

10

0   5   10   15

WRS

23. The Maxwell Land Grant. *Land and Cultural Survival*
(Albuquerque, 1987).

along with those of Governor Samuel B. Axtell, kept the situation in turmoil.

Of Maxwell's unique mansion nothing was left after two destructive fires in the early twentieth century.

Many novels of the West are based on the lives of real men, the truth more or less tailored to meet the demands of fiction. When Harvey Fergusson wrote *Grant of Kingdom*, a novel based on the career of Lucien Maxwell, he had no need to alter the book's major course except to have the protagonist end his life and career on the Cimarron instead of anticlimactically in southern New Mexico. Fergusson's hero, trader Sam Ballard (Lucien Maxwell), marries heiress Consuelo Coronel (Luz Beaubien), and thereby acquires a grant of land measuring sixty by thirty miles, almost two million acres (the Miranda–Beaubien Grant). Characterizations and localities follow the Maxwell model, including the Ballard mansion.

> A great house topping a low hill beside a stream—a house
> large enough to be called a castle, with heavy earthen walls,
> steep shingled roofs and dormer windows, giving it a
> resemblance, which many had remarked, to some of the
> chateaux of northern France. A grove of graceful mountain
> cottonwoods spread their shade around it and over its walls.
> Hollyhocks were pink and white behind the picket fence of its
> dooryard and a plume of blue smoke wavered away from its great
> kitchen chimney. At the foot of the hill many other buildings,
> mostly of adobe, were strung out along a road that paralleled the
> stream . . . In that spring of 1878, Ballard had been established in
> his great house beside the Santa Fe Trail for nearly twenty
> years.[28]

The author has juggled time slightly. Maxwell sold the Grant in 1870, and moved to a ranch near Fort Sumner in southeastern New Mexico where he died in 1875.[29] Fergusson has extended the reign almost a decade. Like Maxwell, Ballard is a cattle and sheep man, and supplier of beef to nearby Fort Union. Also like Maxwell, he is so confident in his power that he can keep twenty or thirty thousand dollars in gold and currency in an unlocked bureau drawer.

Using the personal journals of visitors to the Maxwell domain, Fergusson has written as if he visited there himself.

The evening meal at the house of Ballard was always a social event. Seldom did less than twenty men sit down to the great table. Sometimes there were nearly a hundred and those of minor importance had to wait for a second serving. A truly astonishing variety of human beings passed through that great dining room, for almost everyone who crossed the plains stopped at the Ballard grant. There I met Kit Carson, the most famous scout of his day . . . Lord Dunraven, the famous British sportsman . . . a young German ethnologist, named Bandelier, was another visitor.[30]

The visitors, with the distinguished ones near the head of the table, dined on hand-hammered silver plates, served by Mexican boys. The fare was lavish with "game and beef in great haunches and sides, with trout from the creek and vegetables from the garden."[31] Thirst was quenched with corn whiskey from Taos and red El Paso wine. The women did not join the men at dinner and in fact were seldom seen.

It was a house divided strictly into masculine and feminine parts. There were, in fact, two separate structures, connected by high adobe walls and a small courtyard. The front structure contained the great dining and receiving rooms, and the quarters for all male guests. The rear structure was a feminine world.[32]

This separation of the sexes was a Mexican custom, but at Ballard's (and Maxwell's) it apparently was carried to an extreme.[33]

Lucien Maxwell's ordering of his household along Mexican lines, and even exaggerating them, presents an interesting reversal of the usual practice of Anglos doing things their way. As a particularly strong individual, Maxwell no doubt was comfortable in adopting any custom that suited him, regardless of its origin, and a strict Latin regime in a French colonial house would not have seemed incompatible. In one way the Maxwell mansion was an anomaly, resembling no other domicile of its time and place. In its successful integration of apparently disparate elements of design and construction, however, the mansion not only reflected the complex individuality of its owner, but foreshadowed the dual notes of New Mexican tradition and

Anglo innovation which would characterize domestic building in the Territory for the next half-century.

THE WATROUS TRADING POST

The Maxwell mansion in Cimarron was a stop on the Mountain Branch of the Santa Fe Trail, a fact which accounted for many of the visitors.[34] South of Maxwell's the Branch veered east to rejoin the main Trail in the shadow of the most distinctive natural landmark on the eastern plain, the "wagon mound" (Fig. 24). Visible for miles across the flat landscape, Wagon Mound marked the site of a generous spring, the Ojo de Santa Clara, and a camping ground popular with all, including Indians.[35]

This popularity sometimes caused problems. One of them occurred in the spring of 1850 when the eastbound Santa Fe stage, carrying ten men in its crew and passenger list, camped overnight near Santa Clara spring. While they slept, a band of Apaches silently arrived and hid behind a small hill near the foot of Wagon Mound. The next morning, just as the stage was leaving, the Indians attacked, and in the bloody battle that followed, all the travelers were killed, their bodies scattered as far as seventy yards from the stage coach amid looted debris and ripped mail bags.[36]

From Wagon Mound the Trail continued south to La Junta de los Rios (later Watrous) where, after 1849, Samuel Watrous presided over a thriving trading post. Another trading post, Barclay's Fort, was built at La Junta about 1848–1850, but after spending $28,000 on their sixteen-foot-high adobe walls, Alexander Barclay and Joseph Doyle put the post up for sale a few years later.[37] There were no takers at the time, but after Barclay died in 1855, Doyle sold to William Kroenig. He, in turn, simply abandoned it when he moved to Phoenix Lake in 1879.[38]

The Watrous story is quite different. A Vermont boy, Samuel Watrous came out the Santa Fe Trail with a wagon train about the year 1835. He engaged in several business ventures, married a New Mexican girl, and ran a mercantile establishment in San Pedro. In 1849 he moved his wife, seven children, hired

24. Wagon Mound, a welcome landmark for travelers on the eastern plains of New Mexico, seen from the Santa Clara camping ground. A generous spring, the Ojo de Santa Clara, made this site a popular camping ground for all, including Indians. Photograph, 1979.

hands, and merchandise to La Junta de los Rios, where he prospered. Both the volume of his business and the physical structure of his headquarters grew until the latter was a twenty-five room building surrounding a large patio. The complex included, in addition to the residence, a large store, storerooms, grain and lumber rooms, a blacksmith shop, and so forth.[39]

The house, restored in the 1970s, is impressive. Watrous used resources both local and distant. Of local origin are the adobe walls, rough lumber, and vigas; the iron hinges, locks and grilles were made in his blacksmith shop. On the other hand, elegant finishing items like hand-planed lumber for floors and trim, and window panes, had to come down the Trail, hauled in the big ox-drawn wagons belonging to the freighting firm of Watrous and Tipton.

Those wagons also hauled some of the fanciest furniture and accessories that came to the Territory: the beautiful Vose piano, boxes of books with

> fine leather bindings, the heavy carved Victorian furniture of mahogany and walnut, the marble-topped tables and dressers, the gilt-framed mirrors and gilded clocks. The hand-painted lamps and fine china dinner service, alabaster, shell and brass objets d'art, heavy silver table service and candlesticks, were all brought overland in the great, cumbersome swaying covered wagons pulled by the plodding ox teams.[40]

It was not only the collection of material things that made the scene colorful. When a wagon rolled down the avenue of Vermont willow trees and into the Watrous yard, its drivers were eager to stop and visit with the company they found there: Indians, hunters, Fort Union soldiers, and traders of all sorts (Fig. 25). We have neither diary nor novel to give details of life at Watrous, so must rely on a few historic facts and photographs, and principally on the house itself.

The big one-story house would be imposing anywhere, and at this western crossroads it is remarkable (Figs. 26, 27). It was built with a flat roof, but now has a standing-seam metal-clad pitched roof (Fig. 28). The adobe walls are plastered, accented by shutters. Approaching from the north, a visitor sees a 150-foot long facade with an almost Renaissance quality in its horizontal lines—the row of evenly spaced windows and doors, their strongly defined shutters, sills and lintels, the long, plain, boxed cornice banding the roof edge. Enhancing the classical appearance is the large size of the windows, double-hung with nine lights above and below (Fig. 29). The principal entrance is an attractive, predictable Greek Revival affair: sidelights and transom of small panes, the lower portion of the sidelights panelled; very small pilasters flank the oversize door with its vaguely Greek fret design. The strong lintels of doors and windows are further emphasized by end pieces suggestive of drip molding.

At the north end of this facade is the forty-foot portal which

25. The Watrous Trading Post, 1885. Men, women, horses, carts, and a hay wagon front the Territorial style building that housed the Watrous family and this bustling post. Photograph, Museum of New Mexico.

26. Samuel Watrous House, 1850s. The store portion is at left, with the front portal. Photograph was taken before restoration in the 1970s. Owners' Collection.

27. Watrous House before restoration. The end of the wing at right, with portal and lower roofline, is the first section of the house. The bay window on the southwest corner apparently served as a small conservatory. Owners' Collection.

28. (*Below*) Roofing advertisement from *American Architect and Building News*, August 14, 1880. Metal roofing which came in sections, as in this drawing, could be transported over the Santa Fe Trail in wagons, providing material for terneplate or standing seam roofs before railroad transport was available.

29. (*Facing page*) Detail of door and window, Watrous. Bold, sharply defined lintels and intricately paneled door testify to the care with which the house was designed. Photograph is before restoration, but date is unknown. Owners' Collection.

NORTHROP'S PATENT IMPROVED
SHEET-IRON ROOFING

Is suitable for all classes of buildings, and when properly laid is guaranteed strictly water-tight with a pitch of one half inch to the foot. It is painted with our Asphaltum Oil Paint, a more lasting preservative than a tin-plate, and with occasional re-painting at an average cost of only one per cent per annum,

WILL LAST A CENTURY.
The seams never burst.   The roof is never out of repair.
Send for illustrated circular describing this and our
CRIMPED ROOFINGS and SIDINGS of improved designs, PANELED IRON CEILING, etc.
A. NORTHROP & CO., Pittsburgh, Pa.
Our goods are put on by agents in the tin trade, or where not represented any contracts will be taken by ourselves.

marks the entrance to the store. The portal is stone floored, its roof supported by four small white columns finished with moldings suggesting simple capitals. Double doors lead from the center of the portal into the storeroom (Fig. 30). Watrous's first store had been in the old east wing of the **U**-shaped house, the first section built. This old section presents a very different appearance from the later addition. Also of adobe and with the later pitched roof, the 1849 structure has small double-hung windows with plain framing (Fig. 31).

When a traveler entered the store he found himself in a large room—thirty-five feet by seventeen feet—filled to capacity with

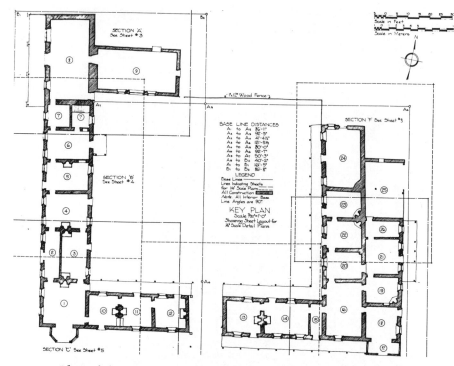

30. Plan of the Watrous House. The zaguán affording access to the courtyard is at bottom center, the older section of the house at right of zaguán. The store with its supply room to the rear is at top left, Rooms 8 and 9. Historic American Buildings Survey.

an inventory to satisfy the needs and desires of the customer: face powder and soap, chest handles and locks, water buckets and milk pails, overalls, shoe polish, whetstones, flannel drawers, mouse traps, cork screws, gingham and calico, wooden butter dishes, needles, buttons and lace, fishing hooks, and so on, in addition, of course, to staples like sugar, coffee, and flour.[41] All this abundance required high ceilings—over eleven feet. The ceiling is of one-inch by six-inch beaded material; the floor is one-inch by four-inch tongue-and-groove. There is no fireplace and the only windows face the portal. Adjoining this room at the rear is a storeroom, thirty-five feet by eighteen feet, with small,

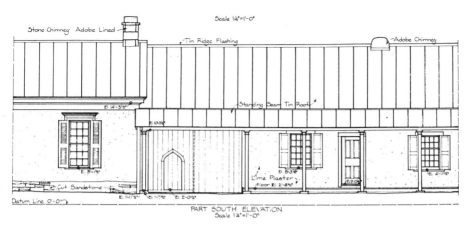

31. South facade, Watrous, showing zaguán. Older wing to the right has lower roofline, smaller windows with plain lintels. The standing seam tin roof replaced the original flat roof. Historic American Buildings Survey.

high windows on the north, barred windows and a large entrance onto the patio.[42] This utility area has a rough ceiling of one-inch lumber, and random width board flooring.

The original store in the east wing had a similar arrangement. Entered from a stone-floored portal on the patio side, it had an almost ten-foot high beaded ceiling, a rough floor and a fireplace. The storage area had only a dirt floor and was accessible for unloading goods through a large, ten-foot-wide opening to the outside, closed by wooden doors.

Corresponding differences are apparent in the finish of the two sets of living quarters. In the original, the fireplaces are typically New Mexican—corner, beehive-shaped adobe; in the newer wing, the fireplaces are of adobe but they are parallel to the wall and have trim wood mantels with classic lines (Fig. 32).

The plan shows the zaguán in the south wing, allowing wagons to enter the patio.[43] Facing south is a small conservatory, its walls composed of small-paned panels of glass. Its ceiling follows the angle of the pitched roof and the beaded one-inch by four-inch sheathing is supported on exposed two-inch by four-inch rafters on eight-inch centers. A ventilating grille is positioned at the top of the wall. Also catching the southern exposure is a large bay window at the end of the later west wing. This bay window contains one-light sashes with large panes, has little distinctive molding as do the other windows of the wing, and probably is of even later date.

Samuel Watrous did more than build an elegant house. *La Junta* became *Watrous* partly because he gave the right-of-way to the railroad and ten acres for a station; he brought the willow switches from Vermont for his avenue; he planted cottonwood windbreaks and an orchard of fruit trees; he put up the first wire fence in Mora County; in 1879 he installed a woolen mill on the Mora River, powered by a water wheel.[44]

The Watrous house represents everything that was up-to-date in domestic architecture in the Territory before the arrival of the railroad, as well it should, for it not only belonged to a trader cognizant of every breath of change that blew across the Santa Fe Trail, but it also was situated within ten miles of a source of great influence on architectural fashion, Fort Union.

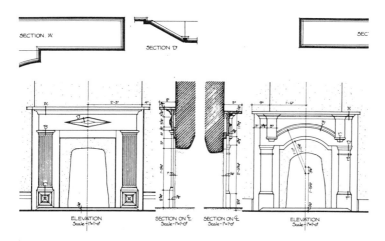

32. Fireplaces at Watrous. Wood mantel of Greek Revival design faces an adobe fireplace, the usual handling in a Territorial house. This change from the corner beehive marks one difference the new style introduced. Date of photograph unknown. Historic American Buildings Survey.

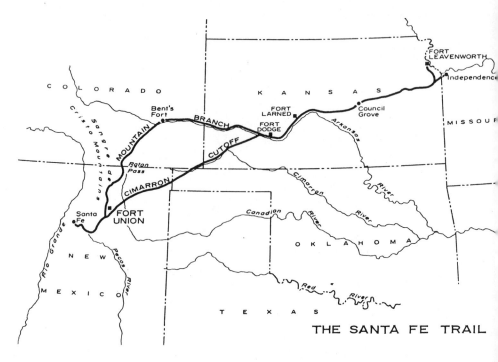

THE SANTA FE TRAIL

33. Map of the Santa Fe Trail. The Cimarron Cutoff, though drier, was shorter and less mountainous than the route through Raton Pass and carried most of the traffic.

3

Forts in Fact
and Fiction,
1860s

Although not falling within the common interpretation of the term *domestic establishments,* the living quarters at Fort Union must be included in this survey because their Greek Revival style and extensive use of technological innovations such as nails and window glass had a powerful influence on domestic architecture in northern New Mexico. In addition, army carpenters and other skilled craftsmen worked with a consistency and precision not always familiar to local builders, and thereby provided those builders with a sense of the possible. While the results were not without flaws, in general the quarters at Fort Union offered a fresh and attractive approach to home design. Fortunately, a number of army wives wrote about their impressions of the fort.

Fort Union was established in 1851 when Lieutenant Colonel Edwin V. Sumner was directed by Secretary of War C. M. Conrad to remove his troops out of the towns of New Mexico and to station them ". . . more toward the frontier, nearer the Indians."[1] One of the principal duties of the army was to protect the Santa Fe Trail, and for this reason the fort was situated near the junction of the Mountain and Cimarron branches of the Trail where the mesa supplied water, grass, and wood (Fig. 33). A distribution point for goods as well as men within a year of

53

its establishment, the fort was a welcome, bustling haven for a westbound traveler such as army wife Marian Russell in 1852.

> At Fort Union our great cavalcade rested. The tired mules were turned out to graze on the prairies. Freight was unloaded and the two hundred horses turned into the corral. Army officers came out and perched on the fence to look over and choose their horses. The parade ground was a shambles of bales of buffalo hides, Mexican blankets and sheep pelts, things to be sent out on the outgoing east bound train that was camped there. Our unloaded freight was piled separately and soldiers were busy unpacking and arranging.[2]

For the next thirty years this energetic community would be the power entity of the area; both militarily and socially Fort Union was a central part of the region's life (Figs. 34, 35).

Even large events might start locally. The Apache War of 1854 was sparked when it was reported that Jicarilla Apaches were plundering the cattle herd of Samuel Watrous, the neighboring rancher who supplied the fort's beef, and a company of dragoons was sent to investigate.[3] This war pitted the soldiers of Ft. Union against the Apaches, and in the years that followed their opponents included Utes, Kiowas, Comanches, Cheyennes, Arapahoes and in 1862, the Confederates. These battles made heroes, and their exploits provide some of the most stirring chapters in New Mexican history: Lieutenant Joseph Maxwell charging up a slope in pursuit of Jicarillas; Colonel Thomas Fauntleroy surprising a Ute village in the midst of a war dance; the battle of Glorieta Pass, when only Fort Union stood between Confederate General Sibley and Denver.[4]

Along with the heroics there were some less savory tales, like the time a soldier gambling in Watrous got in a fight and lost both his money and an eye, and the Christmas Day when "all was quiet until the body of a soldier from Ft. Union was found in the Mora River."[5] One of the spicier stories was the scandal in the summer of 1877, when Miss Lizzie Simpson, daughter of Fort Union's post chaplain, accused the locally prominent Dr. W. R. Tipton of seducing her. The affair allegedly started at a ball at Samuel Watrous's house and continued through a compromising carriage ride and some indiscreet

34. Drawing of the first Fort Union, 1851. Established to protect the Santa Fe Trail, the fort was an important distribution point for men and materials. Museum of New Mexico.

35. Log officers' quarters at first Fort Union. Note stone chimney and Territorial entrance with sidelights and overlight. Some army wives thought these log houses more comfortable than the adobe buildings which replaced them. Date of photograph is unknown, but is probably between 1861–66. Museum of New Mexico.

correspondence on the part of the doctor. The outcome of the matter was that the officer who publicly accused the doctor of the seduction, and who mounted an armed chase after the local man, was himself court-martialed for "conduct to the prejudice of good order and military discipline."[6] The Tiptons were a powerful local family.

Impact from the military installation was not only social but material. The Fort Union Quartermaster Depot was the supply center for the army in New Mexico until the railroad came in 1879, and the wagons of food, clothing, arms and ammunition, tools and building materials that came over the Santa Fe Trail were unloaded at the depot and reshipped to posts to the south and west.[7] Among the building materials that were supplied from Ft. Leavenworth in the years 1863 to 1869 were the nails, window glass, firebricks, and terneplate that went into the construction of new buildings for the fort itself. Much of the material, however, was near at hand. Adobes for the walls were molded on the site; the foundations were native stone; the plaster was fired in lime-kilns south of the fort; the bricks for copings were manufactured in Las Vegas; until the fort got its own planing mill, dressed lumber came from Cerán St. Vrain's sawmill in Mora and two mills on the Sapello River.[8]

The construction method was local, but the style had come over the Trail. Although reflections of the Greek Revival style had appeared in the shape of a few triangular lintels before the United States Army arrived, it was that arrival which was responsible for the invasion of Greek Revival characteristics that would meld with the local Pueblo style to form a new hybrid, Territorial.

When Fort Union was rebuilt after the Civil War, it was built not only in a different location but on a grander scale. Following earlier, cruder quarters, the installation became in 1863–1869 (mostly post–1866) a model of the Territorial style, with its brick-capped adobe walls, elaborate wooden trim, and central hall floor plan (Fig. 36).

Historian Willard B. Robinson suggests the plans of western forts stemmed from the engineering education that army officers received at West Point, and that the forts' construction depended on soldiers and local carpenters.[9] The Greek Revival

36. Quartermaster depot headquarters, Fort Union. Greek Revival details such as the columns, entrance, and lintels, adorning a symmetrical building of adobe walls topped by a brick coping proclaim the Territorial style. Photograph, 1870s. National Park Service.

was an appropriate fashion, neat with a military precision, and the verandas and wide halls proved to be particularly suitable for garrison social life. Buff adobe walls with red brick coping and chimneys, white-painted window facings and lintels, and dark green shutters, a front porch with Greek-inspired square white columns and wide frieze—all these combined to produce a crisp new look in perfect harmony with an old tradition. Windows might be trimmed with either pediment or deep cornice; pilasters flanked the front door and its glass transom and side lights.

Approaching Fort Union from Watrous, the road tops a rise

and there, a mile or so in the distance, is the site of the once big emplacement: arsenal, quartermaster depot, hospital, wagon yard, stables, storehouses, and all the other appurtenances of an active army post, as well as a trim row of officers' quarters (Figs. 8, 37). This line of quarters had a northeast–southwest orientation, facing the northeast, not a particularly felicitous position for the front veranda. However, a north–south placement would have exposed the rear elevations to considerable winds, and east–west would have lost the summer breeze. Probably the most fortunate exposure would have been to reverse the plan and let the veranda face the southwest. An army post, unlike a private residence, could not be tucked under the south side of a hill, as this would leave a blind side to Indians or other unfriendly passersby.

That the quarters were considered pleasant residences by at least some of their tenants is proven by the testimony of the daughter of a post chaplain, Genevieve La Tourrette, daughter of Major James A. M. La Tourrette. (One month after Chaplain Simpson's Lizzie achieved such unhappy notoriety, he was replaced by Chaplain La Tourrette.) In recalling the Fort Union structures, Miss La Tourrette says they were "most comfortable both in winter and summer owing to the very thick walls and spacious rooms."[10] She also has fond memories of social occasions.

> A military wedding is a brilliant affair now, and was in this garrison on the frontier of those days: the large halls being spacious and well fitted for such occasions, the entire hall attractively draped with flags and festoons of greens, the band playing both wedding marches and gay music as we left. Officers wore their full uniforms, and relatives and friends in the garrison as well as from Las Vegas attended.[11]

Not all the ladies assigned to Fort Union were as happy with it. The wife of one commanding officer, Lydia Spencer Lane, had lived in the old log buildings that first housed the fort and preferred them. When Colonel Lane was reassigned to the garrison soon after the new quarters were built, she remarked that "their appearance was imposing, but there was no comfort in them."[12] She approved of neither the floor plan nor the lack of storage facilities.

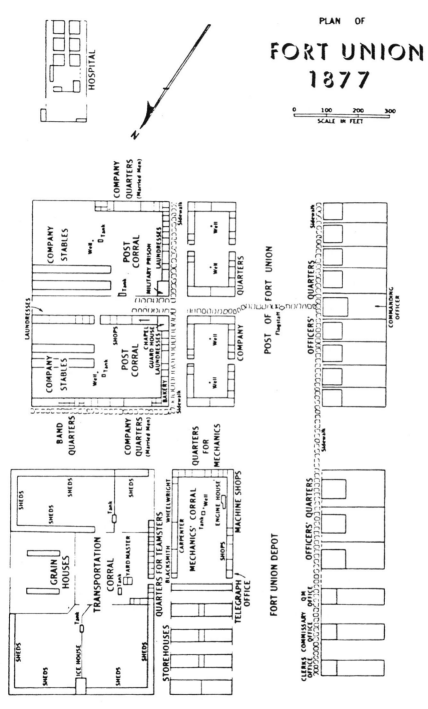

37. Plan of Fort Union, 1877. National Park Service.

The house we occupied, built for the commanding officer,
consisted of eight rooms, four on each side of an unnecessarily
wide hall for that dusty, windy country. They were built of
adobe, and plastered inside and out, and one story high, with a
deep porch in front of the house. There was not a closet nor a
shelf in the house. . .[13]

Mrs. Lane makes a good case for another complaint.

As the plaster dried in our new quarters the ceilings fell one by
one . . . One day I had cooked a dinner for a family of seventeen
. . . It was on the table, and I was putting the last touches to it
. . . I was stooping over to straighten something when I heard an
ominous crack above my head, and, before I could move, down
fell half the ceiling on my back and the table, filling every dish
with plaster to the top.[14]

Miss La Tourette, on the other hand, liked the new house. For
one thing, it was "so well-adapted for entertaining—with halls
extending from the front door to the back, with large rooms
on either side."[15]

Despite Mrs. Lane's complaints, the traditional Greek Revival
center hall plan seems admirably suited both for the double
units which housed most of the officers—apartments of three
large rooms on either side of a common hall—and for the
imposing commanding officer's quarters which encompassed
an entire building (Fig. 38). The commanding officer's quarters
included about 4,000 square feet, the other officers' a maximum
of 1,000 square feet each. The duplexes with both apartments
and the large center hall measure about 2,500 square feet. This
disposition of space was not merely military privilege, as the
commanding officer's share included his office and served other necessary functions of the headquarters.[16]

The central halls used extensively for large gatherings were
about fourteen feet wide, and the one at headquarters was
seventy feet long. In the other residences the shared hallway
was divided into two sections, a long rectangular east section
and a square west section. The commanding officer's house was
heated by four double fireplaces with openings into each room,
and in fact, wood-burning fireplaces or wood stoves provided

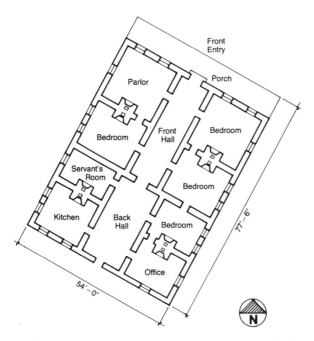

38. Plan of the Commanding Officer's quarters, Fort Union.
National Park Service.

all the heating on the post. Various wells and storage cisterns were the water source; the first installation had relied on a spring for its supply. A foundation of dressed limestone blocks with narrow rubble cores supported the twenty-two-inch thick adobe walls.[17]

Although the officers' quarters displayed a coherent Territorial exterior, the idiom was demonstrated on the interiors only modestly—for example, there are pilasters flanking the fireplace in the La Tourrette parlor (Fig. 39). The classic mode does not dictate the decor. Perhaps a spare and columned Greek Revival interior offered too little comfort on a frontier, and also,

39. Genevieve La Tourrette in the chaplain's quarters, c. 1884. Interior is in the fashion of the day with fringed shawls, crystal prisms, statuettes, and an oriental panel. National Park Service.

there was no pressure to harmonize the interior with the exterior of a home. An 1879 volume on interior decoration "discourages the employment of architects on domestic interiors on the ground that their aim would be to obtain harmony by carrying out in the smaller details of furnishing and decoration the same historical style which they may have chosen for their exteriors, thus depriving household life of a certain part of . . . eclectic individuality."[18]

It is possible to examine parlor decoration at Fort Union because photographs exist of the La Tourrette room in 1884 and of Lieutenant Plummer's quarters in 1888 (Fig. 40). Given

40. Quarters of Lieutenant Edward Plummer, Fort Union, 1888.
The lieutenant does not have a fireplace as the chaplain has, but he
does have a piano. National Park Service.

the difficulty in transporting goods, it seems safe to assume
that there had not been much change for several years previous to the dates of the pictures. The chaplain's parlor is furnished comfortably in the best Victorian style. Flowered carpet
covers the floor (perhaps an area rug as on Lieutenant Plummer's
floor); patterned tapestries dip their fringes to the floor as they
drape little parlor tables. Displayed on the tables are the fancy
lamps and bric-a-brac which give a cluttered, comfortable look.
The mantel boasts a cover edged in ball-fringe, and on it are
crystal-prism candelabra and a handsome clock. Brass andirons
and fender add a glow to the homelike effect. The chaplain's

A. Kimbel & J. Cabus; 7 & 9 East 20ᵗʰ Str. New-York.

41. Queen Anne interior. This 1877 living hall displays the multiplicity of objects and design which was the height of fashion. *American Architect & Building News.*

intellectual bent is suggested by the tall glass-fronted bookcase.

Decor at the Plummer's is less elaborate; he was a lieutenant while the chaplain was a major. In place of an open fire and mantel there is a stove, visible at the extreme left foreground (Fig. 40). The chairs, even the chaise longue, are light, almost insubstantial, as is the little three-legged table with a short cover draped over it. The object of pride is obviously the piano with its scrollwork backed, probably, by fabric. It is interesting that there are no curtains, only the closed outside shutters. The table in the foreground is covered with items such as a lamp with lace and ribbon shade, framed picture, and books.

The Fort Union interiors exhibit some inclination toward the Victorian preference for rooms crowded with diverse elements. In 1831, Englishwoman Frances Trollope admired the trend. "Little tables, looking and smelling like flower beds, portfolios, nick-nacks, bronze busts, cameos, and alabaster vases . . . all the pretty coxcomalities of the drawing room scattered about with . . . profuse and studied negligence."[19] The same style was condemned in the 1880s by Mark Twain scornfully ticking off the bric-a-brac in the parlor of a provincial "leading citizen's house"—"Quartz, with a gold wart adhering; old Guinea-gold locket, with a circlet of ancestral hair in it; Indian arrowheads of flint; pair of bead moccasins, from uncle who crossed plains . . ." along with "sappy" books, seashells, works of art "committed" by the young ladies of the house, and so forth (Fig. 41).[20]

In 1877 *American Architect and Building News* published a series of articles on interior decoration. One of its subjects was a small parlor, in a house of which it says "whatever of architectural character it may have as a whole is due to the inspiration of the Renaissance, but the style is treated without any especial aim at purity."[21] The parlor, *American Architect* goes on to say,

> is to be fitted for furniture in some light-colored wood, and to be decorated with a few paintings in gold frames, vases, plates of faience, objects of bright metal. These must be provided with a neutral background . . . This implies a certain gravity and reserve, an absence of self-assertion. But the general effect aimed at is not one of repose but of animation, with a harmony made up of many elements" (Fig. 41).

Such a harmony prevailed in La Tourrettes' parlor.

On army posts the appearance of the living quarters was not entirely the choice of the current tenants, since practicality ruled that when an officer was transferred it was better to sell the furniture than to move it. La Tourrette mentions that much of their furniture was bought from the previous tenant, Colonel Dent, including a four-poster bed in which, the Dents said, General Grant had often slept.[22]

This fragmentary description of life at Fort Union, and therefore other frontier installations, can be supplemented through historical fiction, such as Paul Horgan's *A Distant Trumpet*, which reflects the period as described in the diaries of army wives.

PAUL HORGAN'S FORT DELIVERY

The trials of life on a frontier fort may be partially reconstructed from the evidence of historical records, but author Paul Horgan has enhanced the record with imagination, and life on a frontier fort in the 1880s is vivid in his novel *A Distant Trumpet*. Against a background characterized by the sweep of space and time that forms the ambience of the American West, Horgan sets his small cast of characters, their daily existence matching that described in the personal accounts of army wives. The result of this combination of imagination and authentic detail provides a feeling for the period that goes beyond historical fact. *A Distant Trumpet* tells a story of a small group in a small place, but at the same time tells cne of the universal stories of the Southwest frontier.

The goals sought and the conflicts encountered during the period of westward expansion in the late nineteenth century differed between the civilian and the military. The United States Army was chiefly occupied with eliminating the Indian threat, thus, insofar as it was concerned, the impacting cultures were not Anglo and Hispanic but Anglo and Indian. In the minds of the military, *Indian* was synonymous with *savagery*; to neither would they have applied the term *culture*. In regard to the Indian, as in so many other areas, Anglos ignored the Spaniards' philosophy. Historian Marc Simmons, contrasting the belligerent stance of the army with that of the Spanish colonial rulers, says that nowhere under the Spaniards "do we find the attitude, so prevalent on the Anglo–American frontier, that the red man stood as a barrier, merely to be brushed aside or trampled under."[23] But the army built its Southwestern forts for this purpose and one other—to bring civilization, as it knew it, to the frontier.

Army life in the latter nineteenth century Southwest was a tangent of Anglo society with traditions of its own, but dedicated socially as well as militarily to this basic Anglo thrust, bringing "civilization" to the West. Exerting influence and force on this effort were not only the region's inhabitants, but also its landscape, its history, and the mystique that clung to the frontier. As a writer striving to recreate life in the Southwest, Horgan explores these nebulous forces and their influence on men's determined drive West.

Referring to the America of the late nineteenth and early twentieth centuries, Horgan says " 'West' was adventure, was romance, was independence, was a new dimension of selfhood."[24] "What dominated all was the splendor of the landscape in its vast scale, its earth features, its colors, its immensity of sky, its rarity of air, and its spacious light."[25] More important even than the mountains and desert, sun and sky, is something else. "Above all, it is the land whose human history, traceable for tens of centuries, seems of all histories which compose the nation's character, the most immediately recoverable in its environment, and yet the most alight with the quality of legend—just as its landscape, made of hard mountains and cruel distances, seems touched with fantasy."[26]

History as part of its environment is a paramount element in Horgan's portrayal of Fort Delivery, set west of the Rio Grande and therefore west of Fort Union, but in a landscape that could lie in eastern New Mexico.

> . . . flat grassy land by the side of a meager creek that ran out of a mountain several miles away to the north. At the creek grew willow trees and cottonwoods to give shade and shelter, and the land bounded south toward grand plains of a desert character. Away off far in that direction other mountains were manifest by day when blowing dust did not hide them.[27]

The buildings, too, are similar to those of Fort Union except for one shingled roof and earthen floors.

All structures are built of adobe, with earthen floors, mud roofs (with exception noted below) and open fireplaces. After heavy rains leaks appear in the roofs and repair is constant. The commanding officer's quarters is the only building with a shingled roof. It is 42 feet wide and 36 feet from front to back. A hall 14 feet wide runs through the center of the house. The front door opens into this from a porch with a low wooden pediment supported by two posts. At the rear of the hall is a back door. From this hall on the left front opens the headquarters office 14 feet wide by 16 feet long. Across the hall on the right are bedroom and dining room in matching dimensions. Ceilings are 10 feet high. The next two sets of officer's quarters consist of three rooms each, while the last set, much smaller, contains one room and a recessed alcove large enough for a double bed.[28]

Fort Delivery is smaller than Fort Union—the latter's arsenal and quartermaster depot triple its size—but life and customs seem to be the same. When the protagonist of the novel, Lieutenant Matthew Hazard, writes his bride-to-be about their future quarters, he says "they offered me #3, also vacant at my arrival, but I decided to move now into #4, as I would only have to shift from 3 to 4 when the C.O. does arrive."[29] In fact, the displacing of another couple from the commanding officer's quarters precipitates a significant scene, a believable circumstance in light of the bitter references to the practice in army wives' journals.

The contrast between what the soldiers and their wives found in the frontier forts with what many left behind in the East is seen in Horgan's description of the bride's home on an army base in Buffalo, New York, where her father occupies the commanding officer's house, the *Castle*.

The Castle was a wide, low house of finely quarried limestone with miniature towers flanking the main door and low crenelations along the lines of the flat roof. Vines clung to its corners and tall elms threw a play of shade over its pale elegance . . . The flower beds were on parade, the white trim of the rosy brick row of officers' quarters and soldiers' barracks gleamed . . .

A long wide central hall was flanked by drawing rooms at the front of the house, and deeper, by a grand dining room opposite to which was the commanding officer's study. A back parlor, pantries and the kitchen completed the main floor. Bedrooms, an upstairs parlor and a sewing room occupied the second floor.[30]

In sharp contrast is the bride's future home.

Adobe, flat roof, thick walls, one room, but with a kind of recess where a big bed could stand. Right now, [Matthew writes] I am still cleaning it out, and having some men paint the walls inside with whitewash, and put glass in the rear window, and fix the front door so it'll actually shut and stay shut. We are sprinkling down the earth floor every day and tamping it to harden it, so the dust won't continually blow up off it.[31]

The furnishings include an iron cot, a table, canvas chair, oil lamp, mirror and basin, and a locker.

Social gatherings at Fort Delivery are arranged much like those at Fort Union. On the occasion of a major general's visit to the garrison, a gala dinner party and dance are held, the ladies wearing the most fashionable gowns they have, and the officers in high full dress. The visiting general, the guest of honor, wears "full-dress blues with long frock coat, two rows of gold buttons, five medals sewed to the breast and heavy dress epaulettes with thick fringes . . . dress boots [with] long spurs nailed to the heels . . . a general officer's gold bullion belt to which was slung a huge saber."[32]

The dinner table matches the diners' splendor. It is set with crystal, silver, linen and lace, candles in silver candlesticks and, centering the table, wild desert flowers in a silver epergne. The menu also is grand, its components partly imported and partly home grown—cold soup, curry of lamb, a salad of fresh cucumbers and French lettuces, melon with the champagne, and German bitter chocolate in gold foil.[33]

After dinner, when the entire garrison joins the party, it could be in Miss La Tourrette's festooned hall.

Out in the long wide hall that ran from front to back of the headquarters there were tentative bursts of music from a violin and a horn, a dimmed riffle on a drum. Subdued but excited talk

hummed over the waiting soldiers and the three women from
Soapsuds Row. On the piazza at the front, the stoop at the rear,
clustered those who could not find places in the long hall . . . At
one end of the hall sat the orchestra—the trumpeter with his
valve cornet, the armorer with his fiddle, and Private Clanahan
with his drum. Three lamps hung in a row down the ceiling.[34]

At Fort Union the company would be fortunate enough to
have a post band, at least in some years, and dances were a
weekly event. For partners the enlisted men depended on the
laundresses from Soapsuds Row and also on the maidservants
from the officers' homes. A problem arose at one time when
most female cooks and housemaids had been replaced by China-
men, the latter being more efficient and not apt to leave to get
married in six months. The soldiers' dances were put in jeop-
ardy for a lack of women, so they bedeviled the Chinese until
the men left, to be replaced by eligible dance partners.[35] Horgan
does not depict such an elaborate social system at austere Fort
Delivery.

In A Distant Trumpet, the rigors of the western plains and
meager comforts of a frontier army post provide more than col-
or. Horgan uses them to support and illustrate one of his major
themes, the contrast between the effete East and the vigorous
West, a concept popular in the nineteenth century. "In the East,
all marvels were man-made, on a scale intimate enough to be
bought or rented, visited or inhabited, in man's dimension. In
the desert West, all marvels were natural ones on a scale so
grand as to make man's survival there an historical triumph."[36]
This grand scale was reduced by mechanical means such as
the railroad, and by man-made marvels like the neat files of
structures at Fort Union, but the immensity, as well as the
railroads and the military presence, played a part in developing
New Mexico.

With homely detail, A Distant Trumpet depicts the flow of
everyday life on the frontier, then enlarges the scene to include
the great forces pressing on that frontier. Fort Union, its army
part of the overwhelming movement West, would also be a part
of the everyday life of future New Mexicans as they walked
across the white-columned portals of their homes, and through
trim, pedimented doorways.

4

Town and Ranch Houses,
1880s

Life in the Territory of New Mexico in the year 1880 was quite different from what it had been twenty years earlier, when Fort Union troops were fighting the Indians and the fort itself was a collection of log cabins. And although there was an increasing amount of communication, it was still different from life elsewhere in the United States. Most westering Americans found it foreign; those from the East Coast found it also primitive and rough. Although exposed to European culture for two centuries, New Mexico had been open to Anglo-Americans fewer than sixty years, a part of the United States for fewer than thirty-five years. It would not be admitted to statehood for another thirty-two, after heated external debate on its qualifications (or lack of them) to join the other states as an equal, along with the debate among its own citizens over the desirability of the move. The transcontinental railroads which had penetrated the Territory in 1879 were working their way south and west, bringing progress and trouble in about the same measure. The east–west railroad meant communication: people and ideas could travel from the coasts to New Mexico in a matter of days, not weeks.

Some of the concerns of the northeastern New Mexican citizen were, of course, the same as those of the Easterner. The New Mexican was interested in politics—the *Santa Fe New Mexican* was supporting James A. Garfield for president, and more important to the local citizenry, Tranquilino Luna for delegate to the Forty-seventh Congress. Also like the Easterner, the New Mexican had to work hard to make a living. For those who had been around a long time, it was ranching or, if they lived in Santa Fe or one of the few other settlements, they might be in one of the professions or the mercantile trade.

The ranching business included not only the sometimes huge sheep and cattle ranches of the plains, but the commerce generated by the stream of herds kicking up a continuous cloud of dust along famous cattle trails such as the Goodnight–Loving, a commerce only beginning to change under the influence of the railroad. A newcomer looking for work might sign on as a cowboy, or clerk in a store, but he more likely would go to the mines.

In 1880 mining was an important industry to the area, and an old one. For hundreds of years Indians had mined turquoise in the Cerrillos Hills; the Spaniards found lead and coal southeast of Santa Fe, and copper in the Santa Rita del Cobre mines. But in the late 1860s, gold and silver discoveries added a brilliant lustre to the hopes of speculators, in some cases justified hopes. Important gold strikes were made in the Mogollon Range in southwest New Mexico and at Elizabethtown in the Sangre de Cristo Mountains of the northeastern part of the state.[1]

For miners, ranchers and townspeople, the business of living in 1880 had its hazards. Runaway teams, domestic squabbles and damaging fires could occur even in the "civilized" regions of the East, but in the Territory they seemed to be more frequent and more disastrous. There was the Las Vegas fire, for example. Las Vegas did not have an organized fire company, and while Old Las Vegas was composed of adobe structures, New Town was built entirely of frame. On September 18, 1880, the predictable happened (in fact the old-town-located *Las Vegas Gazette* had warned against it); half of New Town was destroyed by fire. A sheet-iron stove overturned in W. E. Marble's residence behind his grocery store, and since New Town was built of firewood, so to speak, it went up in flames.[2]

Of hazards endemic to the area, racial tensions ranked high. Even when the issue was not clear, a line between Hispanics and Anglos was apt to be drawn and trouble multiplied, sometimes spreading until the original dispute was forgotten. There were problems that were less strident or less general but still knotty. The land grant controversies had been in the courts for twenty-six years and were still not settled; claim jumpers disrupted the mining community in Cerrillos; bridges washed out; debtors such as John Faber of Santa Fe "took French leave;"[3] railroad accidents were common; hardly a day passed without a barroom brawl or trail argument ending in mayhem.

One problem that exercised the New Mexican newspaper editors throughout 1880 was the "miserably insufficient" mail system. On November 13, in a continuing campaign, an editorial maintained that weekly mail service was totally inadequate for an area of 115,000 inhabitants which had "new settlements and mining camps growing upon every hand, merchants extending and increasing in importance, capitalists coming in every day and investing in property," and "railroads stretching across the whole country."[4]

Not all was strife, of course. On the same day that Governor Lew Wallace announced a $500 reward for the capture of outlaw Billy the Kid, the Santa Fe firm of D. L. Miller advertised that "Mallory's famous 'Diamond' brand Baltimore oysters" were received daily.[5] Along with his oysters the Santa Fe epicure might enjoy a wedge carved from M. Hess Durand's 570 pounds of Swiss cheese, "just received."[6]

Satisfying an appetite for entertainment was the Mitchell Dramatic Company, opening its 1880 winter season in Santa Fe with the drama, *Miss Multon*. Also at home in Santa Fe for the winter were a number of invalids, frontrunners of the health-seekers; even campaigning President Rutherford B. Hayes and his entourage paid a one-day, much-heralded visit.[7]

At least two institutions of learning were thriving in the capital city. At St. Michael's College the tuition and board for the ten-month term was $200, with washing, bedding, languages, and music, extra. (There was an exception to the music fee. St. Michael's was promoting band membership so there was no charge for brass instruments.) The Academy of Our Lady of Light, a finishing school for girls, also charged $200 for tuition and board, but for a young lady to be properly finished the total including extra fees might double that sum: vocal—$20, with harp—$80; drawing and painting—$20; languages—$30; wax flowers—$20; washing, bed and bedding—$20; if she also wished to use the library, though it is hard to see when she would have had time, there would be another $20, bringing the grand total to $410, a considerable sum in 1880.[8]

A restaurant on the Santa Fe plaza, The English Kitchen, offered a single meal for fifty cents, or three-a-day for a week for six dollars. This possibly was too cheap, as the proprietor was the above-mentioned John Faber who ran off to escape his debts.

Material progress was much in evidence. The machinery for a gas works arrived in Santa Fe from St. Louis in September, 1880; merchant Willie Spiegleberg's was the first house to have gas pipes laid, and by December 10, Santa Fe was "a town ablaze with light," the first in New Mexico to be illuminated with gas.[9] In October, 1880, after ten years in business, the Ilfeld Company, the "Santa Fe Wannamakers," moved into a fine new building on San Francisco Street. By the end of the year construction had started on the waterworks.[10]

Such construction itself boosted business, and supported skilled workmen. An advertisement in the *Santa Fe New Mexican* of December 18 called attention to "Monier & Colloudon, Contractors, Stone Cutters and Masons, Santa Fe, New Mexico: Builders of the St. Michael's College and the Sisters' New Chapel."[11] Rope & Castle, a Las Vegas firm, boasted "the largest Stock in the Territory," listing "Doors, Sash & Blinds, Lumber, Lath & Shingles, Mouldings, Pickets, Window Glass, White Lead, Putty and Oil, Roofing Felt, Building Paper, Plaster Paris, Cement, Plastering."[12]

The influx of new people, the railroad shipping capacity, the establishment of lumberyards with doors, mouldings, sashes and blinds, all brought rapid change to one craft which previously had changed but slowly, home building. To a great extent all of the changes could be attributed to the incredible impact of the railroad. Not only did it bring wholesale changes in tastes and goods, but it caused population shifts which spelled the demise of some towns and the birth of others. Along the route of the rails, old settlements shifted their centers—often through the deliberate manipulation of those who stood to make money by such a shift—and entirely new towns sprang up at intervals along the right-of-way like knots on a string.

THE MILLS HOUSE

One of these new communities was the railroad town of Springer on the eastern New Mexico plains. It was founded in 1879 and named for Frank Springer, a lawyer for both the Maxwell Land Grant and the Santa Fe Railroad.[13] In 1881 a traveler from the East, newspaperman C. M. Chase, saw Springer as very small indeed, describing it as having "a depot, two stores, an adobe hotel, a billiard or pool room, and a dozen little houses."[14] The village looked much like its neighbor to the north, Raton, and those to the south, Wagon Mound and Watrous. [15] All had something in common with the 1880 Wyoming town that author Owen Wister describes and deplores as littering

the frontier from the Columbia to the Rio Grande, from the Missouri to the Sierras. They [lie] stark, dotted over a plain of treeless dust, like soiled packs of cards.

Medicine Bow was my first [such town], and I took its dimensions. Twenty-nine buildings in all—one coal chute, one water tank, the station, one store, two eating-houses, one billiard hall, two tool-houses, one feed stable, and twelve others that for one reason and another I shall not name. Yet this wretched husk of squalor spent thought upon appearances; many houses in it wore a false front to seem as if they were two stories high. There they stood, rearing their pitiful masquerade amid a fringe of old tin cans, while at their very doors began a world of crystal light, a land without end, a space across which Noah and Adam might come straight from Genesis.[16]

The railroad towns of New Mexico were smaller, being newer, and might not yet have qualified as "wretched husks of squalor," but they did sport false fronts and no doubt Raton's two saloons would have figured among Wister's unnamed buildings.[17]

Springer, however, could lay claim to an architectural triumph shared by no other town on the plains and one which gave it distinction over its raw-boned neighbors. This was the Melvin W. Mills three-story, Mansard-roofed residence, looming up on the edge of town and still standing in 1986 (Fig. 42).

The owner and builder of the enormous house, Melvin Mills,

42. Melvin W. Mills House, Springer, 1880. North facade displays iron-crested mansard roof and two-story portal, the former a style new to New Mexico, the latter a traditional element. Entrance to Mills's law office was through door at center. Photograph, 1980.

was a Canadian-born, Michigan-educated lawyer who represented a catholic array of clients—the Maxwell Land Grant Company, the Territorial government (as District Attorney for northern New Mexico), and a startling number of notorious outlaws.[18]

Mills's career is briefly outlined in historian Ralph E. Twitchell's *Leading Facts of New Mexican History.* Just a few of the facts indicate the general tone. Much of the action started while Mills was in the wide-open mining town of Cimarron, New Mexico. "The law as administered when the gold excitement was first on was of the 'six-shooter' variety; there were two or three lawyers at the camps but they eked out a living by mining, gambling, or in some way other than the practice of their profession."[19] This apparently was before Mills arrived. One of his first cases was that of a ruffian who invited travelers to spend the night at his remote cabin, travelers who were never seen again. Bags of human bones were found under the cabin. Twitchell explains, "Mills was employed to defend him before a 'mob' jury. The bag of bones which had been found interred in Kennedy's place convinced most of the jury that he was guilty but Mills had two of the jurors on his side and they hung." Nevertheless, Kennedy was lynched that night.

Mills had a varied clientele. Desperados called the lawyer to midnight meetings to solicit his help, and so did the vigilantes who were trying to get rid of them. Active in politics, Mills was involved in a scandalous and bloody election aftermath in 1875 which resulted in his near-lynching. That time he was rescued by the United States Cavalry, and he escaped another lynching through the offices of sometime-outlaw Clay Allison. There are other incidents of mobs and violence, sufficient to make it astounding that Mills died in his bed.

Only thirty-five years old when he built his house in 1880, Mills was already a man of experience and position in the northern Territory, and his numerous enterprises had made him wealthy.[20] After starting his career in Cimarron, he was instrumental in getting the county seat moved twenty miles to Springer when the arrival of the railroad made it apparent that commerce would shift away from Cimarron. Mills's house was Springer's most impressive ornament.

An example of the frontier practice of mixing architectural styles according to whim, the Mills house shows that the method can have pleasantly coherent results. A less successful example of this practice is the Stephen W. Dorsey mansion constructed at Mountain Spring, twenty-five miles to the northeast, between 1878 and 1886 (Fig. 43). In the various phases of construction of the Dorsey mansion, no attempt was made to unify the structure. The major addition, the 1886 stone "castle," was simply attached to one end of the 1878 log house.

The architect of the Mills house is unknown—it may have been the owner himself—but it appears to be the product of

43. Stephen W. Dorsey Mansion, Colfax County, 1878–86. The two-story log house was built at Mountain Spring in 1878, a fine example with dormers, double entrance doors and floor length windows. The stone "castle" was added in 1886. Photograph, 1980.

one unified plan, not a series of additions. Mingling congenial-
ly are Territorial, Mansard, Queen Anne, and a holdover of the
two-story New Mexico mansion, the two-story portal. This
house represents the complete disparity of styles current in New
Mexico just after the arrival of the railroad. It also is one of the
happier examples of a house constructed principally of adobe
but whose design was primarily inspired by Anglo-American
influences.

The two dominating features of the exterior are the cast iron-
crested mansard roof and the two-story encircling porch—the
one borrowed from the French Academic idiom and the other

inherited from Territorial New Mexico. Also Territorial are the pedimented window and door lintels, designed with a unique winged effect where the pediments break up and out (Fig. 44). (Similar flying pediments adorn the Francisca Hinojos house in Santa Fe.) Except for this feature, inspiration for the molded pediment might have come not only from local tradition but from one of the pattern books of the period, such as M. F. Cummings's *Architectural Details*, published in 1873. Most of Cummings's designs are somewhat more elaborate, but nevertheless quite similar to many details of New Mexican houses.

The principal entrance on the south side of the Mills house is double width, its paneled doors arched over with a transom of ruby glass (Fig. 45). Louvered shutters flank the windows, and wood paneling runs under the fenestration of the lower floor. Wood corner facings on both levels suggest simple pilasters. Designs of the two balustrades differ; they, and the porch columns and brackets are neat products of local craftsmen, apparently working with imported models (Fig. 46). The lower balustrade recalls the *stick style* contemporaneously popular in the East. Architectural historian Vincent J. Scully, Jr., describes this style as "the wooden, suburban building of the period 1872 to about 1889," so in 1880 a hint of it was quite up-to-date.[21] Henry Hudson Holly, in his 1878 *Modern Dwellings*, shows similar balustrades as does *American Architect* (Fig. 47).[22]

This fanciful arrangement of balusters was in contrast to earlier New Mexican technique. Two houses completed in the 1850s, Los Luceros in Rio Arriba County and La Cueva in Mora County, were given two-story portals but plain vertical posts in the balustrades. Phoenix Ranch, built in the same period in Mora County not far from Fort Union, received more carefully finished Territorial trim. Its balusters are turned with a moderately elaborate pattern and set vertically.

Foundation and basement walls of local stone support the three stories of the Mills house, the first two floors of plaster-finished adobe. The third, mansard, floor is frame construction sheathed in metal, diamond-patterned shingles, and crowned with a flower border of cast-iron cresting. The mansard treatment is staid compared to many of the possible styles. *Bicknell's*

44. Window detail, Mills. Note flying pediment, similar to trim on the Francisco Hinojos House in Santa Fe, and paneled skirting beneath window. Photograph, 1980.

45. South facade, Mills. Principal entrance has arched overlight in ruby glass spanning double doors. Flying pediment ripples over paired windows. Photograph, 1980.

46. Detail of lower balustrade, Mills. Pattern recalls those of stick style houses, and was probably put together locally, using balusters from a lumberyard. Photograph, 1980.

47. Balustrades in two staircase halls from Holly's *Modern Dwellings in Town and Country* (N.Y., 1878). The one at left gives the effect of the Mills example.

 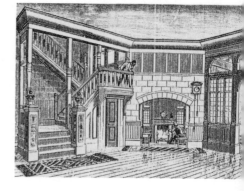

Village Builder, published in 1871, presents a choice of colors and shapes in shingles, and J. W. Fiske of New York, maker of ornamental iron goods, carries a full page advertisement in Bicknell's which offers, among other things, "cresting for mansard and French roofs" (Fig. 48).[23] Fiske mentions that a catalog is available.

This third floor receives light through nine small pedimented dormers, their positions apparently determined more by exterior symmetry and relationship to the chimneys than by consideration of their function (Fig. 49). Cummings shows a dormer design which is very similar to the one used here. Paired modillions support the cornice. Both the cornice and chimney are quite simple.

Admitted through the double doors of the Mills house, a visitor finds himself in an entrance hall bathed in the rosy glow of the red transom, a feature proving the value of the railroad, for such a piece of glass could not have survived the Santa Fe Trail. Both the burl veneer panels of the entrance doors and the regal proportions of the stair newel could have been taken from the pages of another Bicknell architectural pattern book published in 1873 (Fig. 50).[24] Neither is identical to Bicknell's model but is obviously from the same school of thought.

Chef d'ouvre of the Mills interior is the stairway, rising in an uninterrupted spiral from the entry to the third floor, its molded handrail supported by turned balusters. Flat-cut fan motifs finish step ends. This stair spiraling to the third floor was obviously imported from a source at least as metropolitan as St. Louis, as certainly were the doors and probably door casings, though there are no records to prove the origin of these elements. Even if there were an exact pattern for the newel, it appears to be too intricate for local manufacture (Fig. 51).

Also apparently imported is the parlor mantelpiece. Its burl veneer, bosses and plumply rolled lines do not speak of a village carpenter. In older houses, the mantels were simplified Greek Revival, that is, Territorial, when they were not just the corner beehive shape (See Fig. 32). Other interior woodwork displays a less sophisticated flair, but rises above stock molding. In the parlor, the doors are paneled and stained; a line of pearl molding centers the lintel above the transom; corners sug-

48. Mansard roofs often displayed elaborate shingle patterns like this one from Bicknell's *Village Builder,* 1872 (N.Y., 1976).

49. West facade, Mills. The symmetry of fenestration and chimneys seems in strange company with Victorian cresting and dormers, and stick style balustrades. Photograph, 1980.

gest a celtic cross. Window cornices are carefully executed in a vernacular fashion. Floors are wood, walls either wallpapered or plastered. From ten-foot ceilings hang oil lamps, their adjustable chains anchored in decorative medallions.

The house was gigantic for its time and location, although all the rooms are quite small. The thirty-two rooms and hallways were used not only for the Mills household, (which in time numbered seven), but also provided a suite of rooms on the first floor for Mills's law practice (Fig. 52). The north entrance leading to his reception room and private office is lightened by a crossed-circle frieze of openwork on the veranda,

50. Examples of interior entrance doors and newel posts from Bicknell, *Village Builder*, 1872 (N.Y., 1976). Burl paneling and newel shape resemble those features found in the Mills House.

51. Curving stair and elaborate newel, Mills. The stair continues
in an unbroken spiral to the third floor. Photograph, 1980.

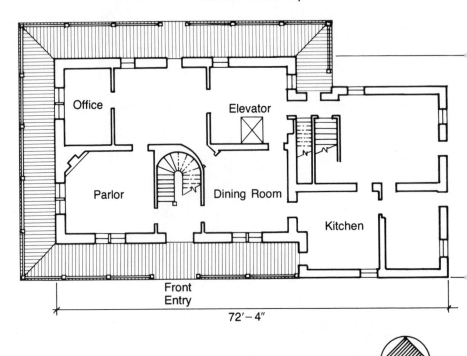

52. Plan of first floor, Mills. Note interior position of elevator shaft, an argument for its having been original. The office was reached through the north entrance. The plan reveals the omission of a *sala*, or drawing room. Historic American Buildings Survey.

another hint of the stick style. Missing from the plan is the grand sala a native New Mexican would have included in such a house.

In addition to the sweeping front stairway, there is a back stair climbing from the five-room basement to the top floor, and in addition, an elevator. Judging by Bunting's findings on elevators in Boston's Back Bay—possibly the most architecturally advanced of the country's residential areas—it seems unlikely that this elevator was original.[25] However, an 1880 installation, with the railroad available for heavy transport, was certainly possible, and the shaft's position in the house might support a case for its original inclusion.

There is an apochryphal tale that offers an additional reason for an elevator having been included when the house was built. The story goes that Mills was in the white slave trade, and that the elevator was used to transport his captives from the basement where they had been smuggled into the house to the third floor. The upper terminal of the shaft is a windowless room, supposedly the victims' prison. Legend further cites a specific case in which a young girl, held captive in this third floor attic, smuggled a note out of the house via a servant. The message reached her uncle—surely her captor cannot have suspected she had a relative within a thousand miles—who clambered up the back porches of the house and rescued her.[26]

Whether or not the versatile Mills included white slavery among his business ventures, the traffic did exist. Miguel A. Otero, writing about the area in the 1870s and 1880s, says

that wholesale trafficking in female human flesh . . . during those frontier days was more horrible than the atrocities committed by the wildest Indians. In order to keep the dance halls filled with girls, the owners would stake some woman to go back East and bring in a fresh lot of girls. They would be induced to come West under the pretext that they could obtain work in some hotel or private family at much better wages than they were receiving in their home towns. But when they reached their destination they would find themselves forced to accept a life of debauchery, or be thrown into the street in a strange town, there to starve to death among the riff-raff.[27]

Mills's various enterprises would have kept him busy without including white slavery. Among his activities he included several ranches, a stock feeding farm, a roofing and paint company, a hotel, a ranch supply store, an insurance business, and stage coach line.[28] His willingness to embrace new ideas was not confined to his house. In a canyon of the Canadian River just below Springer, he planted 14,000 peach, apricot and almond trees, and raised prize fruit until the orchard was destroyed by a disastrous flood in 1904.[29] Eventual political and business reverses deprived Mills of his mansion, and he died a poor man in 1925.

The Mills House is unique. It would have been built at no other time nor place. Only in New Mexico in the late nineteenth century were adobe walls designed to support a mansard roof and cresting, Queen Anne dormers, Territorial pediments on windows and doors, and a double portal with stick-style balustrades. As he did in his professional life, in his house Melvin Mills embraced a lively variety.

THE CHASE RANCH HOUSE

The extravagance of the Mills House was exceptional, of course. A more usual level of comfort and elegance can be found in the Chase Ranch house on the Ponil River, near Cimarron. In the late nineteenth century the Chase house was the headquarters of a 30,000 acre ranch which had been part of the Maxwell Grant. The first four rooms were built in 1871 and the remainder finished in two additions late in 1879. Slightly anticipating the decade, the house nevertheless represents a level of architectural development common to the eighties. A large two-story of twelve rooms, it is constructed of adobe with plaster finish and, unlike the Mills House, has simple wood trim on fenestration and doors (Fig. 53).

It was not surprising that Wisconsin-born Manly Chase built a home more like a midwestern farmhouse than a New Mexican hacienda. Chase first visited New Mexico Territory when he was fifteen, traveling with a wagon train over the Santa Fe Trail. In the Territory again in 1866, he met Lucien Maxwell and the next year, 1867, packed up his wife and worldly goods and moved them to Maxwell's Cimarron country.

Chase's first cabin was on the Vermejo River on about two hundred acres bought from Maxwell. Then in 1869 he bought another 1,000 acres of valley and canyons along the Ponil River, a few miles north of Maxwell's headquarters in Cimarron. Two years later, with two young children and expecting a third, Chase started his ranch hands building a house on his new land on the Ponil. Writer Ruth Armstrong says "it was a simple plan,

53. Chase Ranch House, east facade. Bay window and screening
are additions. Decorative balustrade on porch roof, and lower
balustrade have been removed. Roof was originally shingle.
Photograph, 1979.

just four big rooms, but this would be a real home, not just a
cabin of rough-hewn logs. It would have a kitchen-dining room,
parlor and two bedrooms. The walls would be three adobes
thick, plastered inside and out."[30]

The next eight years brought a rapid increase in the size of
both the Chase ranching enterprise and also the family. By 1879,
Armstrong says, "a steady stream of business and personal
friends came and went through the Chase Ranch, straining the
capacity of four rooms."[31] After her sixth child was born in
January of 1879, Theresa Chase was determined to enlarge the
house even though husband Manly procrastinated. In early sum-

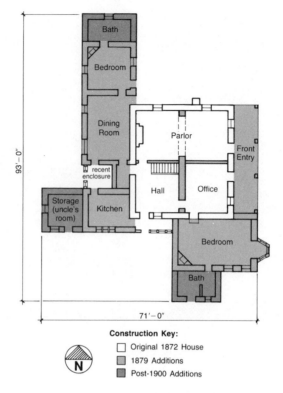

Construction Key:

☐ Original 1872 House
◻ 1879 Additions
◼ Post-1900 Additions

54. Plan of first floor, Chase. All of the first floor walls are adobe except the small porch off the hall. As the key indicates, the original house was a square divided into four rooms.

mer of that year Chase went to Texas to help drive up a large herd of cattle. Armstrong describes Theresa's reaction.

Manly hadn't been gone an hour before Theresa had her plan underway.

She told the workers on the ranch that she was going to add four rooms to the house as a surprise to Manly. She said they must be through before he returned which would be about five weeks. They thought it was a fine idea . . . By the next day the addition was started. The original four rooms had walls three adobes thick on a heavy stone foundation, adequate to support a second

55. Chase House, probably in the 1890s. The porch has both upper and lower balustrades, shingle roof. Owners' Collection.

story. So they simply went up another story, exactly the same size. A steep, narrow stairway went up from the kitchen to a central hallway which opened to four bedrooms. By the time Manly got home it was finished, plastered, the trim painted, floors varnished, and rugs, curtains and furniture in place.[32]

Chase was not angry when he discovered the project, Armstrong states, but ordered the further addition of several downstairs rooms: a new kitchen, bedroom, office, and dining room. "The old kitchen became a foyer, and they knocked out the wall between two of the original rooms, making a large parlor."[33] This is the house that stands in the 1980s with only

56. Chase House, probably about 1900. Decorative balustrade on the porch roof is still in place, but lower railing has been removed. Owners' Collection.

minor alterations. One small bedroom has been added off the kitchen; the original shingle roof is now standing-seam metal; baths have been added as well as a bay window on the east downstairs bedroom (Fig. 54).

Without the ameliorating effects of a mansard roof, dormers, or encircling porches such as the mansion in Springer enjoys, the Chase House projects a solid mass, the primary square block buttressed with one-story adjuncts on three sides. The deep hip roof and the one-story porch on the south subtract little from a four-square effect. Old photographs show white-painted wood-work, a porch balustrade of simple posts, and a further balustrade on the porch roof with crossed boards forming the design (Figs. 55, 56).

Differing from the Eastern-inspired Mills House, the Chase also differs from a traditional New Mexico two-story house. The most obvious difference between it and most two-story ranch houses built by long-time New Mexicans is its lack of a two-story porch or portal. Los Luceros and La Cueva, ranch houses built in mid-nineteenth century in Rio Arriba and Mora counties, illustrate the native New Mexican's concept of a portal (Figs. 57, 58). In addition to porch design, the Chase House departs from local tradition in its plan, which started with a square of four rooms rather than the single row common to the area. The second story for a single-row house completed quite a tall narrow structure, as in La Cueva or the 1912 Max Martínez House in Rio Arriba County (Fig. 59). The latter shelters its double portal under the hip roof.

Windows in the main Chase block are double-hung sash type, with four lights above and below, and are placed symmetrically. Framing for doors and windows is composed of plain boards measuring about one inch by five inches, with two inch by four inch wood sills. Adobe construction would have required a heavy lintel for each opening, but it is not exposed as New Mexican colonial tradition would have dictated.

More important than the exterior to a study of Anglo influences on adobe residences are the interiors of the Chase home. Fortunately preserved much as they were in the late nineteenth century, the interiors reveal no debt to the Southwest, nor even to their position as headquarters of a ranch. The interior walls now plastered were first wallpapered over plaster.[34] An 1899 photograph of the parlor shows it decorated for a family wedding and gives a good view of the frieze enlivening a plain wall (Fig. 60). This arrangement followed a popular fashion, as a discussion of interior decoration in *American Architect* of March 10, 1877, makes clear.

We have discovered that two expressions are required on the walls,—the one brilliant, the other sober,—and that for these there must be provided two separate divisions. It is evident that as the latter element is to furnish a background, it should

57. Los Luceros, Rio Arriba County. This mid-nineteenth century adobe probably was originally one story, but the second floor and two-story portal were added quite early, at least before 1870. Photograph, 1982.

58. La Cueva, Mora County. A much smaller, one-story house built in 1835 was enlarged in the 1860s. The balustrade was of wood, not wrought iron as in this 1979 photograph.

occupy the greater part of the wall-space continuously, and form a screen around the room. The line of division therefore, as the height of the room is sufficient to admit it, must be horizontal. The belt which has the brightness and movement essential to the effect of elegance and animation must be above the neutral screen, and serve as a frieze under the cornice.[35]

Some of the ten-foot-high downstairs ceilings were covered with sheets of metal stamped in designs resembling carving, another current vogue (Fig. 61).[36]

Most floors are of five-inch pine boards. However, a hand-

59. Max Martínez House, Rio Arriba County, c. 1912. The two-story house is only one room deep, its two-story portal sheltered under the hip roof. Photograph, 1979.

6 (7
3 50
0039

some parquet floor was installed in the foyer and parlor as a part of the 1879 remodeling. Adorning this floor is an Aubusson rug bought for the Maxwell mansion and given to Theresa by Frank Springer, one of the officers of the Maxwell Grant (Fig. 62).[37] Later, when the Maxwell household furnishings were sold at auction, the Chases bought several other items, including a dining table and sideboard.[38]

The double parlor created when two of the original four rooms were joined in 1879 recalls a feature of the Greek Revival plan. Architectural historian Talbot Hamlin places the development of a "back parlor" some time after the 1840s. "The rear room

60. Chase front parlor, 1899. The picture was taken when the room was decorated for a family wedding. The arch separates the two parlors. This fashionable interior displays a handsome mantel, wallpaper frieze, and stamped metal ceiling. Owners' Collection.

61. Stamped metal ceiling, Chase. In the late nineteenth century, this material was popular for ceilings as well as exteriors for both commercial and residential building. Photograph, 1979.

62. Chase parlors. Seen from the back parlor, by 1979 the fireplace has lost its overmantel, but retains the lower portion. Aubusson rug was originally in the Maxwell mansion. Velvet draperies beside dividing arch can be drawn to close off the back parlor.

on the main floor throughout this period of the twenties, thirties, and forties was the main family dining room; its use as a 'back parlor' only came in later."[39] By the latter half of the century the front and rear parlors separated only by a partial wall were commonly a part of Greek Revival arrangements.[40] Velvet draperies which can be drawn to close off the back parlor make a sensible statement about severe Cimarron winters.

The parlor fireplace, placed parallel in the center of an end wall, was provided with a carved and decorated mantelpiece and overmantel of wood, the chimney-piece including an arched mirror. Evidence suggests that such an overmantel was con-

63. Chase dining room, 1899. The table is set for the wedding celebration. The room has ample built-in storage along rear wall and a carpeted floor. The wicker highchair drawn up to the table at left indicates that children participated in family festivities. Owners' Collection.

sidered the only desirable treatment at the period. *American Architect*, conducting a competition in interior decoration in 1878, called for a "a chimney-breast and stone fire-place situated at the end of a dining room in a city house."[41] In a group of eight entries to this competition, all had more or less elaborate overmantels, and seven of them included mirrors. In later years, as taste changed, the chimney-piece was removed, but the mantel remains.

In the large dining room the Chases added in 1879, they built a storage wall with drawers and cabinets (Fig. 63). The 1899 photograph shows the table set for the wedding celebration

64. Upstairs bedroom, Chase. These bedrooms have low ceilings and windows, pine floors, and white-plastered walls. Photograph, 1979.

65. At Chase, ornately framed mirror on foyer cupboard reflects narrow stairway. Photograph, 1979.

of Charles Springer, brother of Frank W. Springer, and Mary Chase.[42] According to Armstrong, the menu might have included "oysters, turkey, pâté, candied fruits and nuts, vegetables and pickles from the cellar, bread so delicate it melted in [your] mouth, even champagne."[43] The wicker highchair at the table proves that children enjoyed the family festivities.

The stairway, constructed for use rather than ornament, rises from the foyer to the upstairs hall. It has modest, turned newels and square balusters. The upstairs bedrooms, also, are pleasant but plain (Fig. 64). The stair is quite steep and narrow, a fact that was once mistakenly blamed for a tragedy when sixteen-year-old Maybelle Sherwin was heard to fall and found dying at the foot of the stairway. The culprit was not the stair, however, but a combination of youthful indiscretion and nineteenth century morality. Maybelle, finding herself pregnant by a visiting Austrian nobleman, finally realized he would not return to marry her and had taken a fatal dose of the drug laudanum (Fig. 65).[44]

Like the stairs, the Chase fireplaces were built to be functional. Either wood or coal was burned to heat the house, there being a small coal mine on the ranch.[45] Water was supplied by a water wheel lifting it from the river to a reservoir, then by gravity flow to the house.

The Chase Ranch House, lacking the ostentation of its Mills and Dorsey contemporaries, was exceptionally spacious and comfortable for its place and time. Although it has been solidly at home in its tree-lined canyon for more than a hundred years, it still seems to owe nothing to New Mexico but the material of its walls.

A TOWN HOUSE IN RATON

Some newcomers to the Southwest ignored local building customs entirely and followed the practices which prevailed in the East and Midwest. Their houses were built of wood, brick or stone, not of adobe, and sometimes represented intriguing copies of Eastern models. Among outstanding examples are the George Cuyler Preston House in Santa Fe, a Queen Anne built

66. George Cuyler Preston House, Santa Fe, 1886. An up-to-date Queen Anne design when it was built, the house has stamped metal siding on its second story and the irregular conformation characteristic of the style. Photograph, 1980.

67. William Kroenig House, near Watrous, Mora County, c. 1885. This high, narrow house is of native sandstone and has a standing seam metal roof. Photograph, 1979.

68. House with mansard-roofed tower, Las Vegas, c. 1880. The house next door has a mansard-roofed second story. Photograph, c. 1900, Museum of New Mexico.

in 1886; an imaginative clapboard house with a mansard-roofed tower built in Las Vegas about 1880; and the William Kroenig stone house in the bracketed style built near Watrous about 1885 (Figs. 66, 67, 68). Raton physician Dr. J. J. Shuler built a two-story frame house in the Queen Anne style that illustrates careful importation of both exterior and interior (Fig. 69).

No town in northeastern New Mexico was more dedicated to following the precepts of the States in every facet of life than Raton, on the Colorado border. One reason for this attitude was that it had no Southwestern heritage as a town. It sprang into being in 1879, a result of the railroad's decision that its loca-

69. Dr. J. J. Shuler House, Raton, 1882–96. A clapboard Queen
Anne, the first part of the house was built in 1882. Raton Museum
dates this photograph 1884, but evidence suggests that the
two-story section at right was added in 1896.

tion was better than that of Otero, an already established community five miles to the south (and five miles farther for pusher
engines to travel to the pass summit).[46] After the decision was
made, both houses and commercial buildings were loaded on
flatcars and hauled to the new site.[47] In addition to those structures brought in, the railroad soon built its roundhouse and
shops, and other commercial buildings followed; residential
building lagged (Fig. 70). The population outstripped housing
to the extent that many people lived in boxcars for the first
years. However, as the 1880s and 1890s progressed, more and
more homes were built, most of them striving for the Queen
Anne style.[48]

70. First street, Raton. The Raton Museum dates this photograph
1884. The town was born in 1879 when the railroad moved in a
number of buildings from Otero, five miles south.

Queen Anne, the conglomerate architectural style named for,
but having little to do with, the English monarch of the late
eighteenth century, dominated the fashionable taste of America in the late nineteenth century. Many home builders in Raton
followed the lead, creating more or less successful examples
of houses which "though not looking particularly English, certainly looked like nothing else."[49] The Queen Anne style came
to the Territory on the railroad in 1879 along with Italianate,
Mansard, and Romanesque, but happened to be the latest of
the emigrating styles, so its examples were more nearly contemporary with what was being built in the East, though not
generally as elaborate.[50]

71. House of mixed elements, Raton. Mansard-roofed tower, classic columns, pediment, hipped roof, and balustrade, all wrapped up in imitation stone siding. Photograph, 1980.

One of the primary attractions of Queen Anne was the fact that it had no fixed canons, but encouraged individualism and experimentation. It allowed a mansard-roofed tower attached to the same facade as a double veranda that included classic columns, scalloped shingles, balustrade, and both a pediment and a hipped roof (Fig. 71). A tower might be a small schoolhouse cupola or a large dunce cap. One of the most original expressions of individualism was the six-sided log ranch house built near Raton by the Whistler brothers in 1893.

Among the notable specimens of Queen Anne in Raton is the Shuler House, built in 1882. Dr. Shuler came to Raton in

1881 from Virginia, after medical school in New York and a brief stay in Kansas.[51] He and Mrs. Shuler figured prominently in the political and social life of the town, and their residence eminently suited their position and activities.

The imposing two-story house adheres closer to the Queen Anne idiom than most others of the period, its clapboard exterior expressing a spacious interior of considerable irregularity, one hallmark of the style. The house appears to have had two enlargements, the two-story hall and parlor on the east, and later the second story on the southwest corner (Fig. 72).[52] The first structure may have been simply the doctor's office with small adjoining living quarters.

After the additions, the south (street) front presents a small porch on each floor at the left of a two-story square bay ornamented at the division line by a prominent cornice with dentil molding, and by curved window pediments. An incipient tower capped by a projecting gable dominates the east facade, which is further embellished with an elliptical window and a large piazza finished with a spindle frieze and balustrade. On both fronts the horizontal siding is strapped through the middle by a wide band of scalloped shingles. The roof line erupts into various hips and gables.

The interior realizes the promises of the exterior. From the moment one steps through the front door, the Queen Anne inspiration is obvious; the hall is not only room-sized, about twelve feet by thirteen feet, but is flanked by a fireplace on one wall and a wide staircase ascending the other three (Fig. 73). Thus the entrance hall has all the characteristics of the living hall, though somewhat cramped.

The Queen Anne living hall was required to provide much more than circulation. Scully, in describing its function, says

the great hall creates one large volume, from which the subsidiary volumes branch clearly . . . The hall with its fireplace serves not only as a horizontal and vertical circulation area but also as an open and informal main living area . . . The hall thus becomes the living core of the house and expresses that function in an expansion of space and in a combination of essential architectural and functional elements: entrance, fireplace, and stairs.[53]

72. Shuler addition, view probably dated 1896. A gable-roofed tower form and elliptical window are skirted by a porch with balustrade and spindle frieze. Photograph, Raton Museum.

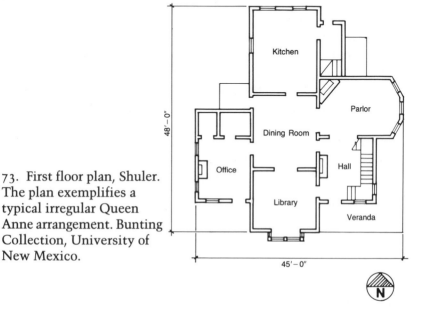

73. First floor plan, Shuler. The plan exemplifies a typical irregular Queen Anne arrangement. Bunting Collection, University of New Mexico.

74. Ware and Van Brunt living hall. The lofty hall has a fireplace under the imposing stairway. Drawing accompanies an article on interior decoration in *American Architect and Building News,* July 21, 1877.

75. Shuler hall, 1897. Although small, the hall exhibits the necessary features of a Queen Anne living hall: entrance, fireplace, and stairs. Photograph, Raton Museum.

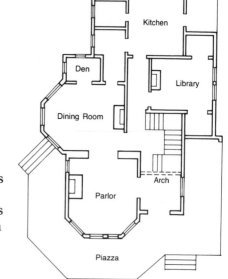

76. House in Albany, N.Y. This plan by Ogden and Wright, Architects, published in 1882, is quite similar to the Shuler plan in both size and spatial arrangement. *American Architect & Building News.*

77. Shuler family in their parlor, 1897. Elaborate mantels in the house are metal, painted in wood or marble patterns. Overmantel has a sentimental Victorian picture flanked by vases; opening to dining room is fitted with ornamental wooden frieze and portiers. Photograph, Raton Museum.

Unfortunately, when modest builders used the living hall concept they ran the risk of creating an area which was "neither fish nor fowl, too big for a circulation area, too small for a living space."[54] There was an enormous difference between the ideal, such as architects Ware and Van Brunt's *Staircase Hall for a Country House*, and what was possible on the western frontier (Figs. 74, 75). However dwarfed in scale compared to the Ware and Van Brunt model, this hall in Raton repeats the model's salient features. Dominating each is the rising and turning stair. The Shuler balustrade is of a more intricate design, but the square, fat newels are similar. In each case there is a prominent fireplace with objets d'art adorning the mantel shelf. Each hall displays wood panelling and is lit by a hanging globe.

The presence of a rocking chair and a doll seen in the 1899 photograph of the Shuler hall indicates that it was used as a living space, and it does serve as a more or less central volume of space into which individual and specialized spaces open.[55] Three rooms extend directly from the hall: the parlor, 12'x15', the library, 13'x13', and the dining room, 15'x13'. That the plan is in the best contemporary style is obvious by its kinship with others of the period (Fig. 76). Behind the dining room is the kitchen with pantries and back stairs, and opening out of the dining room is a door to the doctor's office. Throughout, interior decor and detail followed the Victorian mode with figured wallpaper and carpets, rod-and-spool friezes and bric-a-brac on every horizontal surface (Fig. 77).

The Shuler House, busy with architectural detail and crowded with furnishings, seems quite appropriately at home with Raton's geometrically arranged streets lined by modest residential lots. Neither house and furnishings nor town plan acknowledge that just beyond those neat, small lots lie a hundred miles of almost empty prairie and mountain wilderness. By carefully transplanting their Queen Anne houses to New Mexico, Dr. Shuler and his neighbors created a little garden patch of foxgloves and hollyhocks in the middle of a field of buffalo grass.

With varying degrees of ingenuity and varying measures of success, newcomers to New Mexico in the 1880s imported plans and practices of house building. Some, like Mills and Chase, availed themselves of the local tradition in construction and some, like Shuler, ignored that tradition, but almost without exception their ambition was to duplicate as nearly as possible the aesthetic quality of an eastern rather than a western home.

5

Adobes with Icing,
1890s

As the Martínez, Shuler and Chase houses illustrate, many homes in early New Mexico were built a few rooms at a time, their construction perhaps stretching over decades. This fact often makes it inaccurate to assign a single date to a house. When the building schedule is known, on the other hand, it is useful to discuss a particular house in connection with the period which marked its most significant, or most revealing, phase.

Some of the houses which illustrate contemporary taste and execution in New Mexico of the 1890s fall in this category, such as the Gascón Ranch House at Rociada and the Pinckney R. Tully House in Santa Fe. Others were entirely new structures, such as the Delgado and Shonnard houses of Santa Fe and the Cleofas Jaramillo House in El Rito.

THE GASCÓN RANCH

Gascón Ranch lies in the valley of Rociada, a valley "high, long, and irregular, walled by the higher mountains of the Sangre de Cristo range, east of Santa Fe and the Pecos, north of Las Vegas, away from everywhere . . ."[1] Oliver La Farge, a writer who married a descendent of an early French settler of the Rociada area, describes the beauty of the valley, and its contrast to most of arid New Mexico.

Down the middle of the valley runs a clear, fast noisy stream in which one may take trout. In the lowland along the stream and its tributaries are the farmlands; beyond them are the pastures reaching to the high-wooded knees of the mountains . . . The pasture lands carry grass to tickle the belly of a calf or a colt, or to hide a young lamb. They are mountain meadows, embroidered, according to the season, with iris, columbine, Indian paintbrush, tiger lilies, or cardinal flowers.

When a man who lives and works in the arid country that is most of New Mexico, or even in the semi-green irrigated lands along the sand-edged rivers, comes traveling through such a place as Rociada, he feels his being relax and spread out. He experiences something of what happened to the lotus-eaters, wanting to stay always a little longer, let his horses feast, smell the water, and feel the live grass.[2]

Gascón was named by its founder, Jean Pendaries, who came from Gascony to settle in the valley. He renamed Rociada, which means *bedewed*, because he thought the former name, Rincón, not as lovely as the place deserved.[3]

One of Pendaries's daughters, Marguerite, married José Albino Baca—it was their daughter Consuelo who married author La Farge—and built "a big, two-story adobe building with a pitched roof and porches front and back" at the south end of the Pendaries domain.[4] This house was destroyed by fire in 1962.

Another daughter, Marie, married Richard Dunn, a lumberman from the East, and they made their home at Gascón, a tiny settlement at the northern end of the valley. In the early 1880s they built a two-story frame house, then doubled its size with a one-story addition about 1890 (Fig. 78). In 1925 a log-walled living room was added (Fig. 79).[5]

Although the Gascón Ranch was sold by the Pendaries family before 1920, the house remains in the late twentieth century almost as it was in the late nineteenth century (Fig. 80). The dominating mass is the original two-story gabled farmhouse, its roof line broken by a center cross gable in a design common in the East and Midwest and made familiar to New Mexicans by its use on some of the Fort Marcy officers' quarters built in Santa Fe in the 1860s. A one-story porch follows

78. Gascón Ranch House, near Rociada, Mora County. The main structure was built in the 1880s, though not all at one time. Second floor front porch has been removed. Photograph, 1980.

79. Log addition to the Gascón House was built in 1925. Visible is hiatus in horizontal siding above porch roof, indicating alterations. No doubt original windows matched the longer pair on the other side. Door in center opened onto original porch. Photograph, 1980.

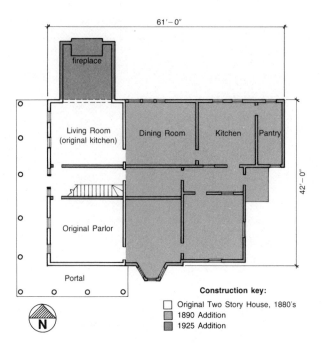

80. First floor plan, Gascón.

the south and west sides, the latter comprising the principal facade. According to family tradition, and the evidence of double doors onto the porch roof from the upstairs hall, the porch at one time had a flat roof and balustrade. Two shorter windows at the north end of the upper story are also apparently of later date, judging by the mismatched siding beneath them.

Long windows fit snugly against the fascia on the second story and against the ceiling of the porch on the first. On the west facade the windows are double-hung sash type, nine-over-six-light downstairs and six-over-six-light upstairs. This constitutes a pleasing difference in proportion, the effect of which is diminished by the overhanging porch roof.

The one-story addition spanning the rear of the house is two rooms in both depth and width, with an offset at the southeast corner and a bay window on the south. The 1925 living room, a gabled, one-story, vertical-log addition, extends north from the original house, its end wall dominated by a native stone fireplace. Except for the log room, the house is finished in dark red-brown horizontal siding trimmed in white, reportedly the 1890 color scheme.[6]

Richard Dunn, the Pendaries son-in-law who built the house, had been in the lumber business in his native Maine, and in New Mexico he continued that occupation along with carpentering.[7] His skills are obvious in this house, which was built of timber cut from the meadow west of the site and dressed in Dunn's own lumber mill. He included details which set the house apart from, for example, the Chase House.[8]

Instead of plain board window enframement as at Chase, the Gascón window frames have a narrow projecting molding capping the window head and an apron beneath the sill. The front entrance is Greek Revival, or Territorial, style with rectangular mullioned sidelights and overlight, the side-lights having a wood panel beneath a six-paned upper portion. In the fixed transom, a double row of four panes ends with two pairs of smaller panes at either side. Slender pilasters flank the door and the entire arrangement is capped by a narrow fascia and cavetto (Fig. 81). Both the screen door and paneled-and-glazed door were apparently bought from a supplier of mass-produced items. The screen door, in fact, could have come from a mail-order house such as Montgomery Ward. (In the 1895 Ward's catalog a very similar screen door is offered for about $1.50.)[9]

The slightly tapering porch columns which rise to a cap suggesting a Doric capital probably were bought rather than made at the site. The bay window jutting to the south at the end of the porch has a paneled base and ornamental scallop beneath its cornice (Fig. 82).

Of exceptional interest in the Gascón interior is the perfectly preserved wood graining, a decorative practice popular throughout the nineteenth century but comparatively rare in New Mexico, though there were some examples in the Palace of the Governors in Santa Fe. As a photograph of the stair shows,

81. Territorial style entrance, Gascón. The screen door might have been bought through a mail-order catalog. Photograph, 1980.

82. Paneled and scalloped bay window, Gascón. Photograph, 1980.

the graining was skillfully executed by an experienced painter (Fig. 83). The technique involves using a brush or metal comb to apply a dark colored graining or glaze over a light base coat. It was used on furniture as well as woodwork and was common enough to require no special instructions to a painter, except as to the variety of wood to be imitated. The following excerpt is from specifications for a house included in Bicknell's *Village Builder* of 1871.

Grain the front and vestibule doors, and all doors and wood work on first story—all to be grained black walnut on two coats of

83. Stair at Gascón. Note painted graining and graceful step end cutouts. Photograph, 1980.

lead paint; grain the kitchen in oak, on two coats of lead paint; grain the shutters to the octagon and dormer windows black walnut, as above mentioned; the newels, hand-rails and balisters [sic] are of black walnut which are to be oiled and made smooth.[10]

Another interior detail of particular interest at Gascón is the wallpaper which is believed to have been applied in the 1890s. Patterns include two vegetable-inspired designs, "okra" and "artichoke," used in the hall and bedrooms, and a leafy print in the parlor. The introduction to the "Wall Paper Department"

84. Victorian accessory, a wall pocket, on okra patterned wallpaper, Gascón. Photograph, 1980.

85. Living room of 1925, Gascón. Everything a dude ranch needs—high ceiling with vigas, native stone fireplace, rifles, fur rug, and, of course, a moose head. Photograph, 1980.

of Ward's 1895 catalog states that "the days of wallpaper as a luxury have certainly gone by when 65 cents will buy enough paper (side walls, ceiling and border) to cover an ordinary size room."[11] The prices in this volume range from seven cents a double roll, for a product "thin but tough," to forty-five cents for "High Art Embossed Paper," a sixteen-ounce paper with "large, exquisitely colored . . . Louis XIV designs."[12] If the papers now in place at Gascón are indeed of 1890 vintage, they must have been of good quality to have endured so well.

Adorning one okra-papered wall is a Victorian accessory called a "wall pocket" (Fig. 84). The Sears Roebuck catalog for 1897

offers three different styles of this item at forty-five, sixty-nine, and eighty cents, and states that "almost every housekeeper knows what a convenient receptacle a wall pocket is," though it does not explain what the pocket was supposed conveniently to receive.[13]

Contrasting with the era of the wall-pocket is the 1925 living room at Gascón. Opening into and thereby enlarging the adjacent room, originally the kitchen, this room appears to display all the appurtenances of the Mountain Cabin: native stone fireplace, moose head, antique firearm, and fur rug beneath an open beamed ceiling (Fig. 85).

Most of the house, however, evokes visions of an earlier day: in the dining room, the table and candelabra remain which were used when the family entertained soldiers from Fort Union; the parlor floor is still covered by narrow-loom floral carpet in shades of rust and green on oatmeal; and, uncomfortably for its occupants, the house is still heated only with wood stoves.

The Gascón Ranch House, built of material gathered and finished at the site, testifies to the result a man experienced with wood could obtain with a minimum of imported items. Although its replica could have been built in upstate New York or some other wooded section of the country, it is a house pleasing to the eye and one whose lines blend with its surroundings. Here, foreign ideas and techniques produced a house which is not alien.

THREE SANTA FE HOUSES

In the capital city of Santa Fe during the last decade of the nineteenth century, citizens were eagerly "modernizing" their homes either from the ground up by building in brick or frame, or by enriching their existing houses with Anglo embellishments. The flat-roofed adobe house was considered not only out of date but a blemish on the landscape. In 1889 *The Santa Fe Daily New Mexican* reflected the prevailing opinion when it editorialized that "occasionally, groves of cottonwoods with darker hues, and shade trees on the streets more completely each year hide the shapeless adobe houses that must give way gradually to modern buildings."[14]

Two houses newly built in Santa Fe in 1890, the Eugenie Shonnard House and the Felipe Delgado House, typify a then up-to-date treatment of an adobe residence, that is, adobe walls plastered smooth beneath a pitched roof and decorated with wood trim (Figs. 86, 87). Another city house, the 1851 Pinckney R. Tully House, was brought into fashion by having its adobe walls painstakingly painted to resemble brick (Fig. 88).

The Shonnard House was built and first owned by a Canadian-born master-carpenter of German extraction, Philip Hesch, and is named for its owner of forty years, sculptor Eugenie Shonnard.[15] The first owner of the Delgado House was a prom-

86. Eugenie Shonnard House, Santa Fe, 1890. Italianate trim adorns this hip-roofed adobe. Photograph, 1982.

87. Felipe Delgado House, Santa Fe, 1890. Residence was above, retail store below. The center balcony canopy suggests the front porch on the Shonnard House. Photograph, 1980.

88. Pinckney Tully House, Santa Fe. Built in the 1850s, the house has been restored to its 1890s appearance, that is, with its adobe wall painted to resemble brick. Photograph, 1980.

inent Santa Fe merchant and trader, Don Felipe B. Delgado.[16] Both of these houses have from time to time been designated as of the Territorial style, but they do not conform to the Territorial idiom in their ornamentation. They are "Territorial" in that they represent a common regional or vernacular vocabulary as expressed in New Mexico of the late Territorial period.

The exterior of the hip-roofed, one-story Shonnard House speaks with a distinctly Italianate (Bracketed) tone. A firmly expressed cornice is supported by paired, scroll-shaped brackets; window heads are emphasized by a projecting, though not

89. Bay window, Shonnard House. Arched recesses enframe square-topped windows under a bracket-supported cornice. Door has arched panels and glazed overlight; porch columns support brackets embellished with molding, bosses, and pendants. Photograph, 1981.

drip-mold, cap. In the bay, arched recesses formed by the masonry extend above square-topped windows, enhancing the Italianate suggestion (Fig. 89). The front porch, whose projecting roof outline might be said to resemble that of a Tuscan tower, bears the most elaboration, especially on its chamfered columns. Connected, solid brackets on the inside corners of these columns create a semblance of arches; outside corners display a profusion of bosses, moldings and pendants. The front door is double with a deep overlight and arched wood panels set off by plump molding. Interior finish is no more than workmanlike, using an undistinguished masonry fireplace and mail-order woodwork.[17]

The lines of the Delgado House, especially of the small second-story balcony structure, are so similar to those of the Shonnard that they suggest the contractor could have been Philip Hesch. The posts and pillar decorations on the upper balcony roof are similar to those on the Shonnard front porch, with the Delgado substitution of ball-and-spindle frieze instead of flat arched brackets. The cornice of the building is emphasized as on the Shonnard House, though because the proportions of the structures differ, it is not as prominent. Its brackets are not paired, but are bulky. Dominating the Delgado facade is a shallowly projecting balcony with a balustrade of close-set turned balusters. Two entrances were provided onto the street, a double door for the ground floor, and a single door leading directly into the stair hall, access to the upstairs.

The Delgado interior is not elaborately detailed. A straight stair has unadorned step-ends and simple turned newel and balusters which could have been bought from a local mill or even ordered by mail.[18] The wood mantels have minimal ornamentation of a Territorial nature, that is, modestly decorated pilasters flanking the opening, and a spare mantel shelf with no chimneypiece. Together the two houses demonstrate a popular way of building in contemporary fashion without entering into great expense; the cake is made with the same ingredients, but the icing is fancier.

The owners of the Pinckney R. Tully House, built in 1851, went to a great deal of trouble in remodeling to make it appear to be a "modern" building. Although originally constructed of adobe, the Tully House was carefully painted to look as if it were made of brick, a more fashionable material.

Tully was a Santa Fe trader who built a nine-room house on his father-in-law's land northwest of the plaza on the road to Tesuque.[19] Within four years, however, Tully left Santa Fe, and the house had a series of owners, none of whom made any significant alterations until the 1880s when a tenth room with a bay window was added. The exact date of its conversion to "brick" is not certain, but it occurred sometime before a photograph was taken in 1890 (Fig. 90).

90. 1890 photograph of Tully House, showing brick pattern on the adobe walls, under a real brick coping. Photograph, Historic Santa Fe Foundation.

The social history of the Tully House covers many high points in Santa Fe's past. After being owned by Tully, the house belonged to publisher Oliver P. Hovey, printer of the first English-language newspaper in the city, and then to William Pelham, the first United States Surveyor General for New Mexico, who made the house his office while trying to verify land grants. Local Santa Fe historian Alice Bullock, commenting on the activities of these various owners, says "one wonders about the content of conversations, plans, even skullduggery that obviously took place at 136 Grant—particularly when the nation was split pro and con on the slavery question and Civil War erupted."[20]

It seems likely that there was even more "skullduggery" discussed in the last quarter of the century when the house belonged to several members of the politically controversial Santa Fe Ring: Attorney William Breeden, Dr. Robert H. Longwill, banker Rufus J. Palen, and Judge Henry L. Waldo. When the house was threatened with demolition in 1972, it was bought by the Historic Santa Fe Foundation and restored to its 1890s appearance.[21]

Unlike the Shonnard and Delgado houses, the Tully House follows much of the formula of the Territorial style: adobe walls, brick (real brick) firewall or coping; pedimented windows; white-painted, Greek Revival—inspired forms comprising its portal. Its kinship to contemporary Territorial structures is obvious in a comparison with the Fort Union officers' quarters (See Fig. 36). The Tully House, however, does not have the central hall plan which often was a characteristic of the style, nor does it have the Territorial entrance of flanking sidelights and fixed transom.

The Tully coping is handsome, a smooth row of brick capping a row laid in crisp dentil design, above two more flat courses. In addition to the full-width portal crossing the east facade, there is a portico protecting a south entrance. Both are distinguished by white painted wood columns, chamfered and treated with capitals of built-up moldings (Fig. 91). On the nine-over-six light, double-hung sash windows, pediment members protrude decidedly. East windows are further accented by exterior shutters (Fig. 92).

The interior of the Tully House was finished with more architectural sophistication than the Shonnard or Delgado houses. The Tully's deep window reveals are wood-paneled, and the Territorial style mantels have tile insertions (Fig. 93). Such ornamental tile was widely used and readily available.[22]

These three Santa Fe structures provide a suggestion of how the taste of urban residents was inclined toward the East at the end of the nineteenth century, and how that inclination was demonstrated when they built or remodeled their homes. The Shonnard and Tully houses, both one-story adobes, differ from each other, but even more severely depart from their one-story adobe predecessors. On all three structures, elements not

91. South entrance, Tully. Photograph, 1981.

92. Front (east) entrance, Tully. Flat arches of painted brick cap pedimented lintels. Entrance lacks usual Territorial side- and overlights. Photograph, 1981.

93. Mantel in Tully House. Fashionable tile facing and hearth pad are in shades of green, tan and rust. Photograph, 1981, during a refurbishing.

native to the Southwest consciously were employed to change, or disguise, the character of the underlying New Mexican adobe house.

AN ADOBE QUEEN ANNE

An interesting facet of the changes that took place in New Mexican domestic architecture in this period is that, almost without exception, each house represented the thoughts of the individuals who first lived in it. There were no large subdivisions designed by a developer or team of architects in which every house shared one amorphous personality. Also, there were materials, tools, and pattern books available which allowed a variety impossible in colonial and early Territorial days. These homes represented the particular tastes of their owners, real people who made choices among the new architectural ideas flowing in from the East.

Few homes of the 1890s made a more personal statement than the Cleofas Jaramillo House. It was built in 1899 in El Rito, near the mid-nineteenth-century house of her mother-in-law, Doña Ana Maria Jaramillo. Upon entering the village of El Rito from the north, on the road that crosses the river, one first sees the older Doña Ana Maria Jaramillo House on the left with its barn and corrals on the right (Fig. 94).

Standing only slightly higher than the river, the old Jaramillo homestead is a long, one-story adobe ornamented with a bracketed cornice and window moldings of an Italianate flavor, along with stained-glass bordered windows and a portal supported by slim, chamfered posts (Fig. 95). Dates are not known for the construction of this house, though part of it may have been built before 1850. It is an enormous house, compared to most homes in the vicinity, but lies close to the ground without ostentation.

Originally there were eighteen rooms, arranged in an unusual zigzag plan.[23] The back wing, nearest the river, housed the ranch office, storerooms, and servants' quarters; the center wing was occupied by the family, and the entire south wing, no longer existing in 1983, welcomed guests. "The guest wing was

94. View entering El Rito. The old Jaramillo House is on the left, their farmyard on the right. The site of the Cleofas Jaramillo House lies in the clump of trees beyond the barn on the right. Photograph, 1979.

95. Doña Ana Maria Jaramillo House, El Rito, c. 1850. This is the central wing; the south wing no longer exists. Photograph, 1979.

96. Cleofas Jaramillo House, El Rito, 1899. Photographed
about 1900, it was quite fashionably Queen Anne. Museum of
New Mexico.

divided into two bedrooms and parlor by blue plush and yellow satin-lined curtains that hung from the ceiling to drag on
the cream-and-blue flowered velvet carpet. Then followed the
guests' dining room, kitchen and living room . . . [with a] grey
marble fireplace in the parlor . . ."²⁴

Just beyond the corrals and field on the west, there was built
in 1899 the surprisingly fashionable Queen Anne home of the
Jaramillo son, Venceslao, and his bride, the former Cleofas
Martínez of Arroyo Hondo (Figs. 96, 97). This second Jaramillo
House stood as evidence of both wealth and indulgence. Not
larger than the parental home—it contained about 5,000 square

97. Jaramillo House in 1979, shortly before it was demolished.

feet—it nevertheless announced the independence and importance of its occupants.

The house was almost square in shape, a single mass capped originally by a straight gabled roof broken only by a center dormer. Within a few years, however, the gables were clipped to form a jerkinhead roof.

Gable ends were framed in horizontal siding above an adobe first story. Molding applied in the Territorial manner trimmed each opening. Columns with bases and capitals constructed of varicolored moldings and a balustrade of short, fat, turned balusters made the front porch particularly appealing (Fig. 98). The

98. Fat balusters and molding-enhanced columns adorn Jaramillo porch. Photograph, 1979.

99. Front entrance, Jaramillo. Door is a mass-produced item, but shaded staining of it reveals it was done by a local painter. Photograph, 1979.

Queen Anne facade was further embellished by stained glass windows, one of which spelled out the motto *Home Sweet Home* in rosy sentiment. Between house and road was a garden containing trees, shrubs, and a rockery.

Such an appearance, in the vanguard of style for New Mexico Territory in 1899, spoke of inhabitants who had traveled enough to know what was fashionable back East (at least as far east as Denver), and who had the means and imagination to combine that fashion with their native adobe construction. Nothing of the exterior betrayed the fact that the second story was a second thought; the structure might have faced Denver's Vine Street instead of a dirt road in El Rito.[25]

The Jaramillos had traveled extensively during the first year of their marriage, in addition to the Denver trips each had made as a child. In her autobiography, *Romance of a Little Village Girl*, Cleofas Jaramillo makes clear the importance of these experiences. Perhaps ingenuously, she gives credit for the design of the second floor of her house both to pictures in a ladies' magazine and to her recollection of hotel lobbies she had admired.

> I . . . showed the builder a picture I had of a house built with a balcony running all around the second story. Four bedrooms and a flower room were added upstairs, opening onto this balcony. That left the large reception hall in the center opened to the ceiling of the second story, in the style of some of the hotel lobbies I had seen.[26]

Beginning at the front door, everything in the house pointed to taste and prosperity. Set into the twenty-inch adobe wall with reveals paneled in the same beige and rose tones of the porch columns, the entrance was framed by the vernacular Greek Revival style of Territorial trim. Unlike this locally contrived surround, the door itself was a mass-produced item with paneling below and its upper clear glass pane bordered by small colored panes in the best Queen Anne taste (Fig. 99). In the 1895 Montgomery Ward catalog, such a door, named the "Garfield Marginal," is listed for $6.68 with plain glass, but the firm could "furnish the above doors, glazed, assorted colored bor-

100. View of living hall from entry formed by lattice, Jaramillo.
Note stairway and upper encircling balcony into which opened
upstairs rooms. Glass panels at rear of hall are not original.
Photograph, 1979.

der lights, with cathedral, enamel or chipped center light, at
an additional cost of 75 cents to the above price of each door."[27]

The door opened into an elegant living hall, a distinguishing
feature of a Queen Anne house.[28] Stretching thirty feet in length,
fourteen in width, with two doors on either side, the hall was
open at the far end to a room which added its depth to the vis-
ta (Fig. 100). Eight feet inside the front door, an overhead spindle frieze with medallions and lattice sidepieces gave visual
separation between the entry and the central hall.[29] This center section rose two stories to a stamped metal ceiling, and was
girdled by a balcony circling the second floor, onto which the

101. Parlor fireplace, Jaramillo. Mantel has oval mirror and tall fluted columns, and was faced with green tiles. Photograph, 1979.

upper rooms opened. An open stair descended from the balcony in two stages.

Although lacking a fireplace, Señora Jaramillo's hall was one of the more authentic living halls to be built in New Mexico. The large room opening off the rear of the hall was the dining room. This area was particularly pleasant; a large, stained-glass-bordered window overlooked the fields back of the house and gave ample light, necessary for the deep interior hall.

Opening off the entry to the right through a five foot wide doorway, the parlor offered the attractions of a fireplace fitted with a coal grate, an oval mirror in its chimneypiece and a fac-

141

ing of small jade green tiles (Fig. 101). This new-fashioned fireplace, like the front door, was one of the contemporary touches which distinguished the house from the older Jaramillos' and from other traditional houses in El Rito. Two windows, each three feet wide, curved around the outside corner in a reflection of a Queen Anne tower. This curve, along with the Home Sweet Home window, lent interest to the 20'x16' parlor. Another charcteristic of the Queen Anne style, a tower might be fully developed or, as here, just indicated by a round or polygonal interruption of an otherwise straight lined perimeter.

Inviting during the summer months, the house was difficult to keep comfortable in winter. The hall and dining room, quite large spaces with no fireplaces, were impossible to heat, and the parlor opened into the hall with no doors. The only room, in fact, which offered the possibility of warmth was the middle room to the left of the hall which possessed a coal-burning fireplace in a fairly small, 12'x15', area (Fig. 102).

What the younger Jaramillos had actually built was a delightful summer house.[30] Any number of people could dance in the two-story hall without getting too hot; for ventilation it was only necessary to open doors to have a breeze from any direction, a much easier and more satisfactory solution than removing a section of roof at each end of an old-fashioned sala. The latter practice is described in connection with a dance attended by Cleofas Jaramillo before her marriage. It was held at La Puente in Abiquiu on the occasion of the marriage of the daughter of the family. "The groom sent two men up on the roof and they swept the earth from two squares, one at each end, lifted the cedar rajas sticks and . . . the fresh air poured down on our heads."[31]

Three outstanding features established this Jaramillo house as Queen Anne: the carefully executed woodwork, the vestigial tower, and the floor plan, which incorporated the Queen Anne living hall into an adobe structure. The hall served its purpose as an elegant apartment for social occasions involving large numbers of people. For the Jaramillos, this might have been a children's party, a square dance, a traveling show with puppets, or a meeting of state or local *politicos*.[32] The plan of the first floor revealed its kinship to a Territorial layout, a wide

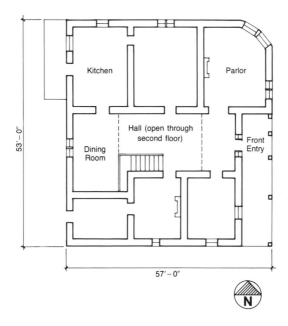

102. First floor plan, Jaramillo. The plan has as much in common with the Territorial symmetry as with Queen Anne irregularity, but the rounded corner and inset porch, coupled with the living hall, are Queen Anne attributes.

center hall flanked by rows of rooms. In this case, the dining room projected somewhat past the center and a rounded parlor corner and inset front porch broke the facade, but the relationship is apparent.

Planned by the owners, the house was built by their neighbors, who included the carpenters and painter responsible for the remarkable woodwork. Most of the ceilings were of beaded tongue-in-groove boards; on the first floor the ceilings were eleven feet high. The wainscot of the balcony was also beaded paneling, with wallpaper above. Otherwise the walls were plastered, except for one paneled side of the dining room.

Cleofas and Venceslao Jaramillo combined their experiences while traveling, their heritage as aristocrats of rural New Mexico society, and their command of indigenous building techniques to construct a home exactly to their taste.[33]

> The house was attractive and lovely. Two carpenters had lavished their skill in the paneling, railings and grillwork. Sam, the painter, had added his artistic talent in penciling wood shades from deep mahogany to cherry red. The wallpaper was of the most attractive and expensive patterns. Little stained glasses surrounding the large panes added color to dining room and parlor windows. Altogether it was an elaborate house with a broad view of green fields, wooded river and purple mountains. It was not so badly planned by two inexperienced twenty-year-olds.[34]

There were other fine houses in El Rito, such as the home of Don Rómolo Martínez, a large, traditionally patio-centered quadrangle.[35] Ten miles southwest of El Rito at Abiquiu stood the fifteen-room mansion of Don Reyes Gonzales and also Don José Maria Chavez's home with its red-carpeted and lace-curtained parlor. Jaramillo describes a visit.

> Cousin José Maria . . . ushered us into a lovely, red carpeted parlor furnished in a black horsehair upholstered walnut suit . . . the beautiful oil lamp hanging over the marble-top center table. The long lace curtains hanging from a fancy brass curtain rod were tied back with tasseled cords. Passing by the old kitchen, used now as a store room, I discovered an interesting type of a fireplace, built in the corner with a *tapanco*, or shelf, over it, where dishes were kept before cupboards were known.[36]

These were classic houses. The Cleofas Jaramillo House was outstanding in its stylishness and its extraordinarily successful melding of "new" Queen Anne elements with traditional adobe construction. This was not merely the usual adobe house with novel furbelows applied to its exterior.

Built at the very end of the century, the Cleofas Jaramillo House was particularly significant. For more than fifty years prior to its construction, architectural fashion in northeastern

New Mexico had moved further and further from the classic adobe until, with this house, nothing traditional remained except the material of the walls. The obvious next phase of evolution would be the elimination of that material.

103. Maestes House, La Madera, Rio Arriba County, c. 1911. One family lived in front wing, another in wing to the left. The pitched roof and pierced porch trim were added about 1914 when a sawmill began operation in the area. Photograph, 1979.

6

*Lodge, Mansion,
and Bungalow,
Early* 1900s

For several reasons, the last dozen years of the Territorial period—1900–1912—offer an anticlimactic final chapter to the history of domestic architecture of the period. First, with rare exceptions such as the 1905 Hobbs House in Raton and the structures at Vermejo Park discussed below, houses became both smaller and less individual, few of them expressing more than conformity to a bland national taste. Second, no stirring account, either factual or fictional, has appeared to lend special drama to the architecture, or even to instill a tangible feeling for the everyday life of that era in New Mexico. Third, the more familiar is more commonplace, of course, and therefore less interesting, and the bungalows which composed the principal style of the 1900s still line the older streets of New Mexican cities and towns.

From about 1900 to the year of statehood, 1912, New Mexicans did not tend to build fine homes of adobe. Almost immediately after this period there began the Spanish–Pueblo Revival, an extremely popular movement devoted to reviving classic building traditions, but in the final years of the Territory, affluent home owners chose to live in houses that bore little cultural relationship to New Mexico. Also in these last years of the Territorial period, some builders began to use the services of architects and to build in recognizable styles other than the traditional Territorial or the elastic and conglomerate Queen Anne.

Of course, houses continued to be built of adobe, especially in rural areas and in urban areas by people of modest means. The Maestes family house near La Madera and the Max Martinez House near El Rito, both in Rio Arriba County, were built about 1911 or 1912 and are large, two-story adobe houses, but their owners were interested in homes large enough for big families, not in being innovative and impressive (Figs. 103, 59).[1]

Important influences on the trend of domestic architecture just after the turn of the century were the rapidly increasing affluence of some local merchants and the beginning of an influx both of wealthy Easterners and Midwesterners seeking New Mexico's salubrious climate, and of artists seeking inspiration. A complex of houses, one of which contains perhaps the single most impressive room in New Mexico, was built on the Vermejo River by one of the health seekers, William Bartlett, a rich Chicago grain trader who brought his ailing son to the region.

A prosperous Raton businessman, Alva Hobbs, used the fruits of a thriving hardware business to construct an exemplary Classic Revival residence. In the cities, the majority of modest houses were designed along the lines of bungalows rather than adobe boxes. Though not typical, because there were few small houses which followed a precise architectural formula, the Harry H. Dorman House in Santa Fe, an example of the American Craftsman style, does represent the general departure from a traditional small New Mexican home. There were obvious examples of other styles. The Greek Revival style appeared in at least two modest houses in Las Vegas (Fig. 104). A number of California-type bungalows line older residential streets in Santa Fe, along with houses of indeterminate, but not Southwestern, heritage (Fig. 105).

ELEGANCE AT VERMEJO PARK

The sumptuous residential complex at Vermejo Park, a large area on the eastern slope of the Sangre de Cristo Range in far

104. Greek Revival Houses, Las Vegas. These small but carefully detailed structures were built between 1902 and 1913. They represent the thousands of tiny Greek "temples" that began to dot America in the early nineteenth century. Photographs, 1979.

105. A Santa Fe bungalow. This residence exhibits ties to California models with its low, broad lines and accents of heavy beams and stone. Photograph, 1982.

northern New Mexico, was assembled by William Bartlett. In 1900 Bartlett read a Maxwell Land Grant Company advertisement offering large tracts for sale.[2] He had a partner, H. W. Adams, in a small cattle operation in Arizona; Bartlett sent Adams to New Mexico to investigate the Maxwell land offer. As a result, by 1902 legal negotiations were complete and Bartlett had bought about 200,000 acres for $195,000, some of it for thirty cents an acre. Adams started a cattle business on the tract. Eventually the ranch included over 300,000 acres, both purchased and leased.

In 1903 Bartlett visited New Mexico with his wife and three

children, one of whom had contracted tuberculosis in 1898. The illness of his son was the motivating factor in the Chicagoan's establishing in New Mexico, in a climate that offered hope for the tubercular.

At the same time, Bartlett engaged Chicago architect J. L. Silsbee to come to New Mexico to supervise his ambitious building program.[3] There would be three houses built, of which the first and largest burned in 1955. A student of Vermejo history, Anne Haslanger, describes this house.

> They called it the "Big House." It had sixty-three rooms. It had a great big **L**-shaped dining room, a huge living room. It was all furnished a la Teddy Roosevelt—big trophy heads, bearskin rugs on the floor, lots of simple oak furniture and lots and lots of liquor. It looked like a hunting lodge; the porch swings hung by chains from the ceiling . . . Mr. Bartlett came summers and he brought lots of guests and that's why they built that big house.[4]

The second structure, built for the ailing son, was called Casa Minor. A photograph of the entire group of houses shows this house as seeming minor indeed next to the huge Big House (Fig 106). The third and most elegant of the buildings, called Casa Grande, was started in 1908 and finished in 1910. Mrs. Bartlett died before construction was begun, and the widower built it "just for himself," with a guest suite for his daughter and her husband.[5]

Casa Grande is an imposing structure of native stone, designed in an eclectic style. The west facade is dominated by a central pavilion whose outline is that of a Flemish gable. In addition to its primary projection, the pavilion's face presents two shallow protrusions, each of only a stone's depth but which cast sharply defining shadows (Fig. 107). The main body of the house and the projecting wing are both hip roofed, but a north gable and a chimney on the east reiterate the Flemish curves.

The roof is of red tile. Low hipped dormers break a boxed eave somewhat awkwardly, especially when the gap is bridged by a gutter pipe. There are a variety of window types, the majority being double-hung sash with sills of cut stone. The top gable arch is repeated in the sun porch windows, however, as well as in an arcaded walkway. A stone-walled terrace punctuated

106. Vermejo Park houses. There were three houses, with the sixty-three room *Big House* at center, *Casa Minor* at left, and at the far right beyond the arcaded walk, *Casa Grande.* Photograph

by huge urns lends formality to the asymmetrical facade. A two-story octagonal greenhouse extending to the southeast accentuates the irregularity of the outline.

The total effect of rough stone, Romanesque arches, Mexican tile and Flemish gables is that of a solidly dignified but nevertheless country oriented lodge, apparently the combination that Bartlett desired. The interior exhibited the same pairing of elegance with informality; Carrara marble columns and a delicately adorned vaulted ceiling presided over bearskin rugs and deep leather couches.

The entrance hall is distinguished by a ceiling elaborately decorated with plaster tracery and rimmed by egg-and-dart molding (Fig. 108). The robust newel supports a bronze statu-

date is unknown, but the *Big House* burned in 1955. Museum of New Mexico photograph by Thomas Fitzsimmons.

ette lamp executed in a manner popular in America at least since the mid-nineteenth century, as the 1859 Morse-Libby stair newel in Portland, Maine, demonstrates (Fig. 109).[7] Hall woodwork was originally dark oak, and the floor small white tile with a sunburst design.[8] The hall leading from the entry was lined with tapestries above the wainscoting.

The plan of the house is more that of a public building than a residence—one dominating space adjoined by several small auxiliary spaces: in this case, entrance hall, breakfast room, sitting room, sun porch, kitchen and greenhouse.

The principal room of Casa Grande is called the library though it no longer contains any books. According to Haslanger, however, it was a true library in Bartlett's era (Fig. 110).

107. West facade, Casa Grande, Vermejo, 1908–10. When the adjacent house burned in 1955, firefighters were able to prevent the fire from spreading through the arcade at left by stacking blocks of ice in it, so legend says. Photograph, 1978.

108. Entrance hall, Casa Grande, as it appeared in Bartlett's day. This photograph, taken about 1912, shows the decorated stairway soffit and fanciful newel light. Museum of New Mexico photograph by Thomas Fitzsimmons.

109. Newel decoration in Morse–Libby House in Portland, Maine, 1859–63. Historic American Building Survey.

110. Original library, Casa Grande. Library clearly has a men's club atmosphere. Glass-fronted bookcases at left are accented by Carrera marble columns. Books also line balcony at far end of room. Museum of New Mexico photograph, c. 1912, by Thomas Fitzsimmons.

When the Bartletts lived here they had an open gallery which
was more library. All around the walls there were bookcases that
were this high, and they had leaded glass doors and they
contained a library of about fifty thousand volumes. On the floor
were bearskins. There were a couple of orientals in here; all
round were very comfortable wing chairs, and just the kind of
chairs that a man would like and it looked just like a man's club,
furnished about the 1910 period.[9]

The Carrara marble pillars were originally imported for use
in a New York bank, but after they arrived were found to be
too short. Bartlett bought them and had Silsbee incorporate
them into the new house. The capitals, which resemble invert-
ed Ionic capitals, were fashioned by a woodcarver from Trinidad, Colorado. All the woodwork in this room, as in the foyer,
was dark oak, including the ribs of the ceiling. The pale plas-
terwork colors have not been changed. (All of the wood was
painted cream and much ornate French furniture was introduced to the house by the W. J. Gourleys in a 1960 remodeling
(Fig. 111).[10]

The library is an enormous room, about 65'x30', with a
twenty-five foot high ceiling. In the center of one side wall is a
fireplace alcove so large it seems more akin to the fireplace of
a medieval hall than to a Queen Anne inglenook. Haslanger
says there were "two couches in front of this fire, and a big
white polar bear skin in front of the fire place."[11] This alcove
is defined by a high arch, twin to another arch at the east end
of the room framing the door to the octagonal greenhouse.

In addition to the library, there is a sitting room which was
also filled with bookcases, and a glassed-in porch where Bartlett liked to play bridge (Fig. 112). From its windows he could
see the Sangre de Cristo Range and the Culebra Mountains of
Colorado—"he owned everything in that direction that he could
see, right to the top of the mountains."[12]

Bartlett built and ran his Vermejo domain like a luxurious
club. He would invite fifteen or twenty guests who came, not
for a week, but for the whole summer. It was a different kind
of lifestyle for New Mexico. Even the ricos had not been able
to afford such luxury and such leisure. There were elaborate
sets of tents pitched at the lake for fishing groups; the Bartletts

111. Casa Grande library after 1960 remodeling. At left is enormous fireplace alcove; arch at far end opens to greenhouse. Photograph, 1978.

112. Casa Grande sun porch in Bartlett's day. He played bridge here in rustic comfort, glancing out the windows at a view of land which he owned as far as he could see. Museum of New Mexico photograph, c. 1912, by Thomas Fitzsimmons.

raised their own squab; they had kennels for airedales and collies; there was a huge wine cellar and a separate house filled with liquor; there was a bungalow for the game warden; they had their own coal mine and electrical system; and after the advent of the automobile there was a fleet of cars. Haslanger gives the following account of life at Vermejo. Bartlett

had cut off from Chicago, become a cattleman. Nobody ever got fired unless he got drunk. Everybody came down from the little mining town of Tercio, sixty miles from this house. At first they brought them in horse and buggies, and they brought the freight

in wagons. The freighter must have made lots of money . . .
everyone was fond of Bartlett. When they ran out of work he
thought of something else. Milk from the Jersey dairy—all the
skim milk they wanted for nothing, other milk was ten cents a
quart. People who worked on the ranch in Bartlett days enjoyed
it. Huge party at Christmas, the men got a new suit of work
clothes. A mechanic's wife got a gold pin with three little
diamonds. The game warden's wife got a series of twenty dollar
gold pieces. The mechanic got a set of German tools.[13]

Bartlett managed his estate as a benign despot for the eight
years he lived there, from 1910 when he left Chicago perma-
nently, to 1918 when he died. After the death of his two sons
in 1919 and 1920, respectively, there were several different
attempts to operate the estate as a private club.[14] In 1948 Fort
Worth businessman W. J. Gourley bought the Vermejo property and increased its size, over the years, to 480,000 acres. The
Gourleys began a guest operation in 1952, using Casa Minor
as their own residence until Casa Grande was remodeled in
the early 1960s. Since 1973, when the estate sold the property
after Gourley's death, Vermejo Park has been owned by an oil
company which uses it as an executive hunting lodge. Much
of the Vermejo land has been given to the state of New Mexico in return for tax advantages.[15]

CLASSIC REVIVAL IN RATON

New Mexican residential elegance in the early 1900s was not
exclusively designed and financed from outside the Territory.
In 1905 a prosperous Raton hardware dealer, Alva Hobbs, gave
the commission for his new house to the regional firm of Rapp
and Rapp.[16] Two brothers, I. H. and W. M. Rapp, headed the
most prominent architectural firm in the Territory, and were
responsible for a number of important structures including the
1905 Y.M.C.A. building in Las Vegas and the 1917 Museum of
Fine Arts in Santa Fe, as well as many residences. The Rapps
worked in a number of styles, as shown by the Spanish–Pueblo

Revival art museum and the Classic Revival Y.M.C.A. An illus-
tration of their interpretation of Colonial Revival is the Hobbs
mansion, employing a High Georgian vocabulary.

The Colonial Revival style, according to an article in *The
American Architect and Building News* in 1881, began with
the Centennial celebration of 1876, although the term *revival*
was not used.

> The year 1876, with its centennial recollections, wrapped us
> roundabout with a mantle of enthusiasm. Suddenly we realized
> that we were born of a line of heroes who had founded a nation;
> our cupboards and attics were ransacked for relics of the past;
> Chippendale furniture and Dutch clocks resumed their sway;
> Delft plates adorned our walls, and houses were built and
> restored with every attempt to render them as much like those
> of the last century as possible . . . Let us therefore study the
> principles that shaped and guided the architecture of the colonial
> period and the first fifty years of American independence, not
> merely to find quaint details to copy in modern work and then
> unblushingly christen those works Queen Anne or Georgian, but
> humbly and earnestly . . .[17]

This discussion of styles linked the Queen Anne with "colonial" types; the article's first heading reads "Queen Anne and
Georgian architecture, giving their origin and the causes which
have led to their renaissance."[18]

Only a few years later, however, the Queen Anne had fallen
from favor, at least among architectural critics. Its position was
being superseded by the growing popularity of colonial tradition and of the Classic Revival, a movement for which the 1893
Chicago World's Fair had generated great enthusiasm. William
Nelson Black, writing in the *Architectural Record* in 1892, even
sees some professions exemplified in the classic mode and
"erratic Queen Anne cottages."[19]

> Were one authorized to apportion the houses of the town among
> the inhabitants for places of residence we would feel inclined to
> give the dwelling with the Greek portico, or facade, to the
> county judge and his accomplished family of grown-up sons and
> daughters, and one of the Queen Anne cottages to the veterinary
> surgeon.[20]

Black's principal point, however, is that the use of wood for classical details is unsuitable. He says that

> the architect cannot ever attempt to give expression to his sentiment of grandeur in wood without becoming in a measure, and in a pretty large measure, too, ridiculous . . . Those massive columns in wood are too suggestive of sections of the mast of some tall ship to be in keeping with the architectural style of a people who build of stone or marble . . . wood is really a suitable material only for buildings that make no architectural pretensions whatever.[21]

This was not a universal opinion, and there continued to be built houses of wood with considerable architectural pretensions.

One of these is the Hobbs House in Raton. Of frame construction finished in horizontal siding, it was quite in the mainstream of residential building with its classical columns and pilasters of wood. That the Colonial Revival embraced a High Georgian style complete with classical columns illustrates the elasticity of the term *colonial* (Fig. 113).

The Hobbs mansion is High Georgian in both mass and effect, though not archaeological. The two-story rectangle has a Georgian hipped roof interrupted by two dormers in front and one in the rear. The house features several of the devices characteristic of the late Georgian style: a robust cornice and wide frieze, corner pilasters capped by Ionic volutes, porch columns with Doric capitals, arched dormer pediments, and a Palladian window. A one-story porch spans the facade, distinguished by a projecting center section and balustrades. Balustrade members are square but relieved by inset sunburst motifs on the upper level, as well as hearty corner posts topped by finials.

The rear elevation presents a glassed-in sun room (a popular feature immediately after 1900), capped by a balustrade, and irregular fenestration including a Palladian window. With this exception, windows and doors pay no tribute to classicism (Fig. 114).

The Hobbs floor plan reveals a confusion of styles not unusual for a period of transition, a Queen Anne inglenook at odds with its primarily classical surroundings (Fig. 115). A plan published in *American Architect and Building News* in 1900 is quite

113. Alva Hobbs House, Raton. The house with its Classic Revival facade facing south, is painted yellow with white trim accenting columns, balustrades, pilasters, cornice, and dormers. Photograph, 1980.

similar, though the designer refrained from including an inglenook and doubled the proportionate size of the central hall. This Ottumwa, Iowa house was of "narrow clapboards, painted Old Colonial red" and was, like its Raton counterpart, adorned by corner pilasters, classic columns, a Palladian window, and balustrades.[22]

In the Hobbs House columns and pilasters with Ionic capitals separate the large entrance hall from the parlor. The rather steep stairway has simple balusters and a newel formed by a swirl of the balustrade. Opposite the parlor is the dining room dominated by a deep inglenook complete with built-in fireside

114. Rear elevation, Hobbs. This elevation shows a Palladian window over the stair landing and irregular fenestration. Glassed-in porch at right was a popular feature immediately after 1900. Photograph, 1980.

115. First floor plan, Hobbs. A fairly classic design is interrupted by the dining room inglenook.

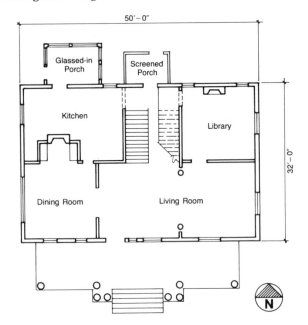

116. Inglenook in dining room, Hobbs. The high, dark wainscoting is offset by floor length windows on the facing wall. Photograph, 1980.

benches (Fig. 116). A high wood dado surrounds the room, an effect lightened by a bank of floor-length windows opposite the inglenook. In general the rooms of the house do not seem adequately spacious to complement the exterior elegance, particularly on the second floor, which is a jumble of five bedrooms and narrow halls. Heterogeneous interior details include beamed ceilings and glass-fronted bookcases.

Although designed by regional architects, the Hobbs House reveals no regional characteristics. It was built during that period in New Mexico when Old Pueblo and Territorial styles were outdated and the Spanish-Pueblo Revival had not yet begun.

The house remains a splendid example of the Colonial Revival fashion, handsome in any part of the country and exceptional in New Mexico.

A SANTA FE BUNGALOW

As is true of every time and place, of course, for every mansion built there were built many cottages, and like the mansions, the cottages reflected contemporary fashions. Northern New Mexico was not immune to the bungalow epidemic which swept the country in the early 1900s. *Bungalow*, a word applied to a type of one-story house, is a term which came from India where it denoted a low structure with a thatched roof extending over a veranda.[23] After the concept reached the United States, a number of developments combined to create the American bungalow.

An Arts and Crafts Movement had been initiated in the mid-nineteenth century by British social philosophers and men of the arts such as John Ruskin and poet and painter William Morris.[24] As the name implies, the movement encouraged the use of handcrafts and natural materials, and insisted on simplicity in domestic design. The movement's influence traveled to America, resulting by 1897 in the organization in Boston of the first American Society of Arts and Crafts.[25] From the other side of the world, Japanese concepts were introduced which complemented the arts and crafts idea. At the Philadelphia Centennial Exposition the public saw for the first time Japanese carpenters at work. Architectural historian Marshall B. Davidson describes the public's reaction.

> Those who came to gawk at the exotic customs and outlandish costumes of the Oriental workmen remained to admire what they contrived with their nimble hands and traditional equipment. The straightforward, organic design, the "honest" woodwork construction, the open planning, and the discreet decoration of Japanese architecture were all features that appealed to those looking for an escape from the staid formalities of Victorian fashion.[26]

It was simultaneously with these trends, and partly in rejection of florid Victorian houses, that the shingle style and stick style developed, mentioned above in connection with the 1880 Mills House at Springer. Houses in these idioms were much less contrived and encumbered than most Queen Anne architecture.[27] Frank Lloyd Wright expressed his objection to the superabundant "trimming" and "joinery" which made a house

> a bedeviled box with a fussy lid . . . Floors were the only part of
> the house left plain after "Queen Anne" had swept past. The
> "joiner" recommended "parquetry" but usually the housewife
> and the fashionable decorator covered these surfaces down
> underfoot with a tangled rug collection because otherwise the
> floors would be "bare." They were "bare" only because one
> could not very well walk on jig-sawing or turned spindles or
> plaster ornament.[28]

Credit for the amalgamation of the influences which produced the bungalow is usually given to Charles S. and Henry M. Greene, architects practicing in California in the 1890s and early 1900s. Architectural historian David Gebhard summarizes their landmark structures.

> Their Bandini House (Pasadena, 1903) was a single-floored,
> U-shaped house oriented around a courtyard; while their Ford
> House (Pasadena, 1904) grouped its two-story space around a
> completely enclosed patio. By 1907 in the Blacker House
> (Pasadena) and in 1908 in their famous Gamble House
> (Pasadena), they had fully established the style of the "woodsy"
> California bungalow, with its low-pitched, widely over hanging
> roofs, extensive porches and terraces, its "open" plan extending
> outdoors, and its use of "natural" material: shingles, untreated
> wood, brick, and stone. The style was seized upon by builders
> and developers and by the late 1910s, entire districts of
> American cities were covered with small and large versions of
> the California bungalow (Fig. 117).[29]

In fact, the Greene houses do not look much like most of the bungalows which covered entire districts. The prototype was one-story with a pitched roof, and a front porch supported by

117. Blacker House, Pasadena, California. The 1907 Blacker House was considered a fully established example of the California bungalow as executed by architects Greene and Greene. Greene & Greene Museum, Pasadena.

heavy, square, tapering columns of fieldstone, brick, concrete or wood.

There were a number of variations of the bungalow as there are of its successor, the ranch-style house (Fig. 118). There were "Mission Style" bungalows and "Greek Revival" bungalows, and some in a mode named for a magazine which supported the Arts and Crafts Movement and urged its readers to learn simple home repair and maintenance, the *Craftsman*. The *Craftsman* was edited by Gustav Stickley, who with his fellow editor Edward Bok of the *Ladies Home Journal*, was a disciple of William Morris.[30]

118. Variations on the bungalow. Both in Santa Fe, one of these bungalows has Mission Style arches, the other uses an uncommon adaptation of a Greek attic on a flat-roofed bungalow. Photographs, 1982.

The appeal of the bungalow was its simplicity, use of hand—worked natural materials, and low cost. New Mexico already had a house type which filled those requirements, and for the area filled them more satisfactorily, but the bungalow was built in the Territory for another reason; it was the house that was being built in the rest of the United States.

Quite a few bungalows of various types survive in the towns of northern New Mexico. One of the best preserved examples is in the Craftsman manner, built in Santa Fe in 1911 for amateur photographer Harry H. Dorman. The mass of the Dorman house is characteristic of a bungalow, essentially a square with a short wing at the rear, the roofline consisting of a main gable, subsidiary gable on the wing, and a dormer (Figs. 119, 120). The original roof was of sawn redwood shingles, its deeply overhanging eave further declaring the style of the house.[31]

The facade lacks the predictable ponderous front porch, employing instead a more graceful arrangement of a terrace covered by an open row of beams. The supporting cross-beam rests on round posts topped by zapatas, the only hint of the Southwest to be found in this structure (Fig. 121). The prominent beams recall work by the Greenes, such as the Blacker House.

Resting on a foundation and partial basement of ashlar-coursed limestone, the walls of the main floor are brick and those of the gables of frame and stucco. Exposed rough wood makes robust natural window framing, and emphasizes the gables and dormer in bold verticals between panels of stucco. Although reminiscent of the exposed members of a stick style house, the effect suggests more forcefully the look of Japanese shoji screens, as the house expresses strong horizontal lines rather than the vertical statement of the stick style.

In plan the Dorman bungalow is representative. The front door opens directly into the living room, a radical and money-saving change from Queen Anne, where even the great halls themselves had entrance halls (Fig. 122). The living room opens into the dining room without separating doors, still the most common disposition of space in a ranch house. Although *bungalow* implies only one story, bedrooms were often built into the gables, as in this case. Stairs were objects of utility rather than beauty, and were small and unobtrusive.

119. Harry Dorman House, Santa Fe, 1911. These 1913 photographs show the west (top) and east facades of the Craftsman bungalow. Museum of New Mexico photograph by Jesse L. Nusbaum.

120. Dorman House. View shows west (principal) facade at left with open beams spanning the terrace. Photograph, 1982.

121. Exterior detail, Dorman. Beams covering west terrace are supported by posts and *zapatas*. Exposed structural wood carries out Craftsman theme. Photograph, 1982.

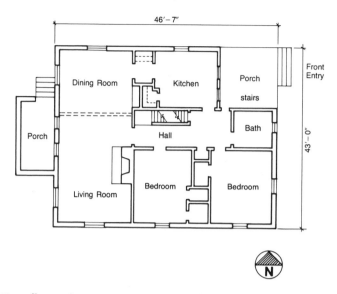

122. First floor plan, Dorman. A typical bungalow plan, living room opens directly to the outside and to the dining room; stairway is minimal.

By definition a bungalow is simple, but the Dorman interior boasts some features that go beyond simplicity. Plaster panels framed in wood form a high wainscoting in living and dining rooms (Fig. 123). A round-arched Richardsonian brick fireplace and a carved and arched door dignify the living room (Fig. 124). A built-in china cabinet in the dining room displays square lines compatible with other woodwork in the house, all of which, with the exception of the door, is perfectly unadorned.

The gardens, situated in an orchard that dates before 1870, were restored in the 1980s, and again include walls and paths delineating swaths of lawn and beds of informally massed flowers.

123. Dorman living room, 1913. One of the virtues of the bungalow is that it makes a house seem more spacious than its dimensions suggest, as in this view through the living room and into the dining room. Museum of New Mexico photograph by Jesse L. Nusbaum.

124. Arched door and fireplace, Dorman. Features of the living room have the sturdy natural look of the Arts and Crafts Movement, but their simplicity approaches sophistication. Photograph, 1982.

The Dorman House, along with some other small homes in New Mexico in the early 1900s, was well conceived and executed. In addition, there were a few exceptional residences, like the Hobbs House in Raton and the houses at Vermejo Park, built during the period. However, these examples could not compensate for the loss of a regional architecture which, partly because of its suitability to the terrain and climate, lent a peculiarly warm quality to New Mexico's towns and rural spaces.

For the most part, in place of vernacular adobes, streets were lined with rows of bungalows just as in any other part of the United States. Paradoxically, as this conformity became nearly complete, a new movement began to form which would reverse the direction of architectural fashion, sending it back toward the New Mexican house of adobe, flat roof and vigas.

7

Enduring Adobe

Architecture is a response—a response to the demands of an environment that encompasses not only the exigencies of weather but also the vagaries of men. During the Territorial period, New Mexican architecture responded to the pressures of invasion, both of ideas and materials. For a while, these pressures seemed to be stronger than those indigenous to the region. But in the 1910s and 1920s, after almost a century of decline, interest revived in the traditional architecture of the Southwest. One explanation of the resurgence of the adobe house is a mud wall's intrinsic identification with the land, and the land's pervading influence.

Perhaps the principle reason that the Southwest has been inhabited by humans for more than 1,500 years is that although its mountains and deserts have a forbidding grandeur when viewed from a distance, it is hospitable to men. The climate is mild but has enough character to be interesting; water is scarce but not absent; and while the land may not burst with abundance, it will respond to cultivation. Over the centuries this hospitality has remained tempting, and newcomers as well as old timers have succumbed to it.

Beside these practical virtues, the Southwest, including New Mexico to a marked degree, has a mystique that exerts a strong hold on the susceptible. The source of this mystique has been attributed to a number of elements—the Indians, the mixture of cultures, the brilliant sunshine, the ages of human habitation. Efforts to communicate a sense of the mystique can be found throughout the literature that discusses the area. Even though Fray Marcos in 1539 was motivated by anxiety, it is interesting that a pueblo built of rock and mud could seem to him "a very beautiful city . . . the houses . . . all of stone, with their stories and terraces . . ."[1] Historian Marc Simmons suggests "that the clear, rarified New Mexico air, heightening the illusionary effects of light and space, played its trick and showed the eager Franciscan what he wanted to see."[2]

In later years, an author sometimes knew he was under a spell. Charles F. Lummis, the anthropologist and journalist whose 1893 *Land of Poco Tiempo* first called widespread attention to the region, begins his book with "Sun, silence, and adobe—that is New Mexico in three words . . . It is the Great American Mystery . . .'Picturesque' is a tame word for it. It is a picture, a romance, a dream, all in one."[3]

Socialite Mabel Dodge Luhan, a devoted immigrant to Taos, writing in 1951, feels strongly about the town's acceptance or rejection of strangers.

> If they come and do not fit into the good spirit of Taos, they do not stay. They cannot. Nobody tells them to go away, they just disappear. The "genius loci" of the Valley is benign and tolerant and it maintains a creative direction. Anyone who, in his essential nature, opposes this spirit of the place is forced out by it, for it is very powerful.[4]

Luhan, who moved to Taos in 1916, is representative of a group who made New Mexico their adoptive home, beginning as early as the 1890s with the arrival of a few artists to Taos. Almost simultaneously with the final disappearance of interest in the adobe house as far as the general population was concerned, that is by the mid-1910s, this group of artists, archeologists, writers, and patrons of the arts (of whom Luhan was one) began to express renewed concern with preserving the traditions of the Southwest, including the adobe. Their interest was to some extent a statement of the larger "back to the land" impulse, part of which was the Arts and Crafts Movement mentioned in connection with the Dorman bungalow.

Although for the most part the newcomers were people of

modest means, Luhan was an exception. In the late 1910s she built a large and unique house in Taos, where she presided over her salon in the West, luring to her drawing room some of the best known names in the artistic world. The Luhan House, although far too large to be a typical residence, is of adobe and was designed in a traditional way, that is, by drawing lines in the earth showing where the walls were to be.

It was during the period of about 1910–1920 that the re-born building style was crystallized and came to be called the Spanish-Pueblo Revival.[5] At first signifying respect and admiration for the old buildings as they were, the Revival developed a momentum of its own, and in some cases tended to prefer them as they should have been.

The 1920s–1930s immigrant to New Mexico, even one who had slender resources, had two attractive alternatives if he had the current predilection for the old, the traditional, and the simple. He could, for very little money, buy an old, traditional, and simple adobe house, sweep it out, hang curtains, set up his easel and paint. Since the object would be to live a life of basic values he would not miss indoor plumbing or artificial heat. For a larger investment but still a reasonable sum, he might build a new, traditional adobe, almost as simple but with a few amenities. There were guidelines to help him, and detailed discussions of the idiom as in Sylvanus Morley's article, "Santa Fe Architecture," published in 1915 in the periodical *Old Santa Fe*. But many artists enjoyed designing their own homes.[6] In general these new houses shared with the old the box shape, small rooms, and small windows, sometimes adding superfluous detail, too many *corbels* and *nichos*.

In addition to these more or less casual builders, there were talented artists designing in the Spanish-Pueblo mode, notably sculptor Carlos Vierra, who built a spectacular house in Santa Fe. Also, there were a few practicing architects like the firm of Rapp and Rapp who built the most influential structure of the Revival, the Museum of Fine Arts in Santa Fe, and John Gaw Meem, architect of many residences and public buildings in the style.

As the region's attractions became more widely known, it prospered, and the houses became more elaborate. Some of

Meem's are quite large, perhaps five thousand square feet, and contain expensive details of hand-carved wood and hand-wrought iron. It was a fairly common practice to incorporate in a new or remodeled building architectural elements from older structures. An ancient door or beam might be referred to as "rescued" or "pirated," depending on the point of view of the speaker.

An unfortunate result of the momentum of the Spanish–Pueblo was the forcing into its mold buildings of other styles. A neat small Greek Revival bank on the Santa Fe plaza was stripped of pediment and columns and given a blank, adobe colored facade with a portal flounce. After the Staab House, a two-story 1888 mansion also in Santa Fe, lost its mansard roof and had its first floor smothered by a Spanish-Pueblo addition, it became an architectural embarrassment.

Overall, the Revival was of great benefit, preserving a unique ambiance. The zeal to make every building conform to Spanish-Pueblo was principally confined to Santa Fe and Taos, with a few devotees in other areas of the state. The fervor abated somewhat after mid-century, as respect grew for styles such as Greek Revival, Queen Anne, and even the bungalow, which represented other phases of area history.

Over the years, New Mexico has been impacted by a series of social movements or states of mind. To both the Spanish and North Americans it was first a frontier, offering land, power, and adventure to such as Don Severino Martínez and Lucien Maxwell. To the Spaniards, it also presented an opportunity to reap a harvest of souls for the Catholic Church, and an unrealized hope for a harvest of treasure in gold and silver. To a lesser extent the Spaniards pursued the rewards of trade, but the latter were the riches that beckoned entrepreneurs like Watrous and Mills. New Mexico lured not only missionaries and adventurers. The area's salubrious climate always attracted the sickly, at least as early as 1831 when Josiah Gregg was advised by his physicians "to take a trip across the prairies, and in the change of air and habits . . . to seek that health which their science had failed to bestow."[7] Each of these invaders brought his own ideas about houses, from the Spaniard's molds for building blocks to healthseeker Bartlett's Flemish gables.

The adobe dwelling survived these intrusions and alterations.

Architectural critic Rex Newcomb gives three tests of a good house, "(a) Is it logical and appropriate to its environment? (b) Is it well planned—efficient as to its utilities? (c) Has it beauty of line, form, and colour?"[8] The adobe house meets these requirements in full measure—logical because made of the earth it stands on, an appropriate material which endures in the dry climate and insulates against the heat and cold: efficient in that its one level opening to the outside utilizes that outside, and expansion is merely a multiplication of existing forms: beautiful and serene in its repetition of the line, form, and color of its surroundings.

However appropriate, the adobe gave way for a period. There were alien forces pressing against its walls, leaving their imprint in the mud, eroding its foundations, molding and finally replacing it, to conform to the philosophy of its inhabitants. In every period, homes reflect changing times and the evolving ambitions of their owners; in the structures of no other time or place is the history of a society in transition more subtly but clearly written, than in the houses of the Territory of New Mexico.

Notes

P R E F A C E

1. This book does not attempt to deal with Indian and early Spanish colonial architecture. For these periods, as well as further discussion of the Territorial period, see Bainbridge Bunting's *Early Architecture in New Mexico.*

2. Brooke Hindle, "How Much is a Piece of the True Cross Worth," *Material Culture and the Study of American Life,* ed. Ian M.G. Quimby, 6.

3. Hindle, *Material Culture,* 10.

4. Ivor Noel Hume, "Material Culture with the Dirt on It: A Virginia Perspective," Quimby, *Material Culture,* 33.

C H A P T E R 1 *Introduction*

1. Bunting, *Early Architecture,* 27.

2. William A. Keleher, *Maxwell Land Grant: A New Mexico Item* (Santa Fe: Rydal, 1942), 5.

3. Marc Simmons, *New Mexico: A Bicentennial History* (N.Y.: W.W. Norton, 1977), 84.

4. Jessie Bromilow Bailey, *Diego de Vargas and the Reconquest of New Mexico,* (Albuquerque: University of New Mexico Press, 1940), 208.

5. Simmons, *New Mexico,* 9.

6. Donald Jackson, ed., *The Journals of Zebulon Montgomery Pike* 1.(Norman: University of Oklahoma Press, 1966): 391.

7. W. W. H. Davis, *El Gringo: or New Mexico and Her People* (Santa Fe: Rydal, 1938), 100.

8. Charles Gritzner says that "it is possible that highland areas of northern New Mexico have the greatest concentration of historic log buildings remaining today anywhere in the United States." "Hispanic Log Construction of New Mexico," *El Palacio* 85:4 (Winter, 1979–80): 21.

9. Bunting, *Early Architecture*, 1.

10. Davis, *El Gringo*, 40.

The houses are built of adobes, or mud bricks dried in the sun, and are but one story in height; and there are only two two-story houses in the place, neither of which was erected by the Mexicans. The walls are much thicker than those of a stone or brick house, and, being of drier material, they are cooler in summer and warmer in winter than the former. The almost universal style of building, both in town and country is in the form of a square, with a court-yard in the center. A large door called a zaguan leads from the street into the patio or court-yard into which the various rooms open. A portal, or, more properly, according to the American understanding of the same, a porch, runs around this court, and serves as a sheltered communication between the different parts of the house. The roof is flat, with a slight parapet running round it, which adds somewhat to the appearance of the building; and the water which collects upon it is carried off by means of wooden spouts that extend into the street . . . The only wood used about the roof is the sleepers and the boards laid across them to hold the earth, because of the high price of timber. They cover the sleepers with a foot or eighteen inches of dirt, which they pack down, and then besmear it with a top coating of mud to make it water proof.

11. Bunting, *Early Architecture*, 14.

12. Susan Shelby Magoffin accompanied her husband on a trade expedition to New Mexico in 1846. She was, as she proudly noted, the first American woman to enter Santa Fe under the American flag; in her journal she recalls her vivid impressions of the foreign country.

13. Susan Shelby Magoffin, *Down the Santa Fe Trail and Into Mexico: The Diary of Susan Shelby Magoffin 1846–47*. Edited by Stella M. Drumm (New Haven: Yale University Press, 1926; rev. ed., 1962), 23.

14. Davis, *El Gringo*, 51. Davis goes into more detail concerning the method of construction:

The internal arrangement of a Mexican house is as different from that of an American as the building itself. The style is essentially Spanish, blended with which are observed many traces of the Moors, their early ancestors. As has been remarked before, all the rooms open into the patio, except some which communicate directly with the sala and with each other. It is a very rare thing to see a board floor in a Mexican house, the substitute being earth, cheaper in the first place, and more easily repaired. A coating of soft mud is carefully spread over the earth, which, when dry, makes a firm and comfortable floor. The common covering for the floors, when they are covered at all, is a course article of domestic woolen manufacture, called gerga, which answers the purpose of a carpet. The inside walls are whitened with calcined yezo or gypsum, which is used instead of lime, but it does not adhere to the walls with the same tenacity, and comes off upon every article that touches it. To prevent this, the rooms are lined with calico to a height of four feet, generally of bright colors. The coating of mud and yezo on the inside of the house is generally put on by females, who make use of their hands and a piece of sheepskin with the wool on for that purpose, instead of brushes and plasterer's tools.

15. Davis, *El Gringo*, 164.
16. Magoffin, *Down the Santa Fe Trail*, 154.
17. Davis, *El Gringo*, 203.
18. Davis, *El Gringo*, 185.
19. Magoffin, *Down the Santa Fe Trail*, 60.
20. Magoffin, *Down the Santa Fe Trail*, 61.
21. Stanley F. Crocchiola, *The Watrous, New Mexico, Story* (Pantex, Texas: n.p., 1962), 9.
22. Davis, *El Gringo*, 175.
23. Louise Harris Ivers, "The Architecture of Las Vegas, New Mexico." Dissertation, University of New Mexico, 1975, 295.
24. Oliver La Farge, *Santa Fe: Autobiography of a Southwestern Town* (Norman: University of Oklahoma Press, 1959), 86.
25. Marcus Fayette Cummings and Charles Crosby Miller, eds., *Victorian Architectural Details: Two Pattern Books by Marcus Fayette Cummings and Charles Crosby Miller. 1868, 1873* (Watkins Glen, N.Y: American Life Foundation, 1978), plate 48.

CHAPTER 2: *Two Haciendas and a Trading Post, 1820s–1850s*

1. A more detailed discussion of building methods is found in the Introduction, above.

2. Bainbridge Bunting, *Taos Adobes: Spanish Colonial and Territorial Architecture of the Taos Valley* (Santa Fe: Museum of New Mexico Press, 1964), 5.

3. Bunting, *Early Architecture*, 63. New Mexican historian Myra Ellen Jenkins feels the Indian threat was not sufficient in the Taos area in the early nineteenth century to have required fortifications. Interview with Jenkins, February 18, 1982.

4. Bunting, *Taos Adobes*, 23.

5. Bunting, *Taos Adobes*, 24.

6. Ward Alan Minge, "The Last Will and Testament of Don Severino Martínez," *New Mexico Quarterly* 33: (Spring, 1963): 50. The measurement, *vara*, is the equivalent of "nearly 33 English inches." Josiah Gregg, *Commerce of the Prairies: The Journal of a Santa Fe Trader.* 1844 (Dallas: Southwest Press, 1933), 145.

7. Minge, *Last Will and Testament*, 51, 52. The reference to planked floors appears to have been an error in translation. Bunting says "except in the remodeled entryway, Room 13, the house never had wooden floors." *Taos Adobes*, 25. Even in the Governor's Palace in Santa Fe there was not a wooden floor as late as 1846. Bunting, *Early Architecture*, 81.

8. Bunting, *Taos Adobes*, 24.

9. Bunting, *Taos Adobes*, 24.

10. Bunting, *Taos Adobes*, 24.

11. Harvey Fergusson, *Grant of Kingdom.* 1950 (Albuquerque: University of New Mexico Press, 1975), 31.

12. Bunting, *Taos Adobes*, 24.

13. Magoffin, *Down the Santa Fe Trail*, 154. See Magoffin's comment in Notes for the Introduction, number 12.

14. Fergusson, *Grant of Kingdom*, 34.

15. Minge, *Last Will and Testament*, 54. Don Antonio José Martínez (Padre Martínez) figures largely in nineteenth century New Mexico history as a powerful force in the Taos area.

16. William A. Keleher, *Maxwell Land Grant: A New Mexico Item* (Santa Fe: Rydal, 1942), 27–29.

17. Sytha Motto, *Old Houses of New Mexico and the People Who Built Them* (Albuquerque: Calvin Horn, 1972), 20. This source tends to be anecdotal.

18. William A. Bell, *New Tracks in North America: A Journal of Travel and Adventure Whilst Engaged in the Survey for a Southern Railroad to the Pacific Ocean During 1867–8. 1870* (Albuquerque: Horn & Wallace, 1965), 108.

19. Colonel Henry Inman, *The Old Santa Fe Trail : The Story of a Great Highway.* 1898 (Topeka: Crane, 1916), 374.

20. Inman, *Old Santa Fe Trail,* 375.

21. Lawrence R. Murphy, "Master of the Cimarron: Lucien B. Maxwell," *New Mexico Historical Review* 55:1 (January, 1980): 7. The Menard house is a standard of the French vernacular influence in its area.

The French colonial house on the site of Fort Kaskaskia was built in 1802 by Pierre Menard, presiding officer of the first territorial legislature and the first lieutenant governor of Illinois. Even though France lost all territory east of the Missisippi to England following the Treaty of Paris in 1763, French cultural influence continued for many years. The Menard House, with its basement floor of masonry and its first floor exterior of oak protected by a porch on three sides, is a fine example of the lingering French vernacular. G. E. Kidder Smith, *A Pictorial History of Architecture in America,* vol. 2 (N.Y:American Heritage, 1976), 436.

Hugh Morrison says: "Even the year before the Louisiana Purchase, a fine French Colonial house was built by Pierre Menard on the river bluff below Fort Kaskaskia, its low-pitch hipped roof spreading wide over a thin-posted *galerie* of airy lightness." Hugh Morrison, *Early American Architecture: From the First Colonial Settlements to the National Period* (N.Y: Oxford University, 1952), 259.

22. Inman, *Old Santa Fe Trail,* 376–377.

23. Inman, *Old Santa Fe Trail,* 376.

24. Agnes Morley Cleaveland, *Satan's Paradise: From Lucien Maxwell to Fred Lambert* (Boston: Houghton Mifflin, 1952), 7.

25. Cleaveland, *Satan's Paradise,* 7.

26. "A Bostonian's View of Cimarron," *Cimarron News and Press,* 28 July 1881.

27. The Maxwell Land Grant fight, which gave rise to the Colfax County War, occurred as a result of the allegedly crooked amplification of the 97,000 acre Miranda-Beaubian Grant into a 2,000,000 acre Maxwell Grant. It is the subject of many articles and books, including William A. Keleher's *Maxwell Land Grant: A New Mexico Item* (Santa Fe: Rydal, 1942).

28. Fergusson, *Grant of Kingdom*, 64.
29. Murphy, "Master of the Cimarron", 20.
30. Fergusson, *Grant of Kingdom*, 79.
31. Fergusson, *Grant of Kingdom*, 79.
32. Fergusson, *Grant of Kingdom*, 79.
33. Fergusson, *Grant of Kingdom*, 80.
34. Inman, *Old Santa Fe Trail*, 376–377.
35. The village may have been called either Santa Clara or Pinkerton in 1880. "The Village had been called Santa Clara . . . (P.O. 1876–77) later changed to Pinkerton (1881–82) and finally to Wagon Mound (1882). pop. 1882, 300." *Comprehensive Plan: Wagon Mound, New Mexico: New Mexico Project P-66*, prepared by Kenneth W. Larson and Assoc., City Planning Consultants, Albuquerque, 1970, 1.
36. Hobart E. Stocking, *The Road to Santa Fe* (N.Y: Hastings, 1971), 289. The official report of this incident may be found in *The Official Correspondence of James S. Calhoun*, ed. Annie Heloise Able (Washington, D.C: U. S. Government Printing Office, 1915), 206–207.
37. Crocchiola, *Watrous*, 11. For a detailed and fascinating biography of Barclay, see George P. Hammond's *The Adventures of Alexander Barclay: Mountain Man* (Denver: Old West, 1976).
38. Alice Bullock, "Watrous: A Living Relic Where Rivers Meet," *The New Mexican*, undated clipping in file of New Mexico State Archives, Santa Fe, New Mexico.
39. Motto, *Old Houses of New Mexico*, 53.
40. Motto, *Old Houses of New Mexico*, 54.
41. Springer Letter Book, February, 1884–September, 1884, from the Charles Ilfeld Company Papers, Special Collections at Zimmerman Library, University of New Mexico. These items are mentioned in the correspondence and are assumed to be representative of the items in the store.
42. That this was an entrance is a supposition based on the practical need for a storeroom. The openings had become windows by 1980.
43. The patio in 1980 could be entered from the north through a gate, but the old walls, now razed, indicate that this was not the case during Watrous's time.
44. Motto, *Old Houses of New Mexico*, 53.

C H A P T E R 3 : *Forts in Fact and Fiction, 1860s*

1. Robert M.Utley, *Fort Union National Monument, New Mexico*, National Park Service Historical Handbook Series No. 35 (Wash-

ington, D.C: U. S. Government Printing Office, 1962), 9.

2. Garnet M. Brayer, ed., *Land of Enchantment: Memoirs of Marian Russell Along the Santa Fe Trail* (Evanston: Branding Iron, 1954), 28.

3. Utley, *Fort Union National Monument*, 14.

4. Utley, *Fort Union National Monument*, 16, 18, 25.

5. Crocchiola, *Watrous*, 14.

6. Patricia Y. Stallard, *Glittering Misery: Dependents of the Indian Fighting Army* (San Rafaela, Cal: Presidio, 1978), 111–113.

7. Utley, *Fort Union National Monument*, 50.

8. Utley, *Fort Union National Monument*, 35.

9. Robinson, Willard B. *American Forts: Architectural Form & Function*, 1977. (Ann Arbor, Mich: Books on Demand, University Microfilm International).

10. Genevieve La Tourrette, "Fort Union Memories," *New Mexico Historical Review* 26:4 (October, 1956): 1.

11. La Tourrette, *Fort Union Memories*, 4. Utley also describes this sort of occasion:

Weddings were gala affairs, with the preparations absorbing as much enthusiasm as the ceremony and attendant festivities themselves.

If a regimental band happened to be stationed at the post, balls were regular and well attended. "The quarters at Fort Union" recalled an officer's wife, "had an unusually wide hall which was superb for dancing, and three rooms on each side. We had only to notify the quartermaster that a hop was to be given, when our barren hallway would immediately be transformed into a beautiful ballroom, with canvas stretched tightly over the floor, flags decorating the sides, and ceiling so charmingly draped as to make us feel doubly patriotic." The men turned out in dress uniforms, the women in ball gowns fashionable when last they had been stationed in the East. Led by the impressively dignified bandmaster, the musicians poured forth marches, waltzes and polkas. Between dances, the men gathered with cups and cigars at the punchbowl. Often the festivities ended only with the approach of reveille.

Utley, *Fort Union National Monument*, 56–57.

12. Lydia Spencer Lane, *I Married a Soldier or Old Days in the Old Army*. 1893 (Albuquerque: Horn & Wallace, 1964), 143.

13. Lane, *I Married a Soldier*, 143.

14. Lane, *I Married a Soldier*, 146.

15. La Tourrette, *Fort Union Memories*, 3.

16. Headquarters were used for official entertaining, for example. See following section on Paul Horgan's *A Distant Trumpet*.

17. Utley, *Fort Union National Monument*, 10, 36.

18. The volume referred to, reviewed in *American Architect and Building News*, February 8, 1879, 43, is the following: *Art in the House. Historical, Critical and Aesthetical Studies on the Decoration and Finishing of the Dwelling.* By Jacob von Falke, vice-director of the Austrian Museum of Art and Industry at Vienna. Authorized American, translated from the third German edition. Edited with notes by Charles C. Perkins (Boston: L. Prang & Co., 1879).

19. Mrs. Frances Trollope, *Domestic Manners of the Americans.* 1832. Edited by Richard D. Heffner (N.Y: New American Library, 1956), 338.

20. Samuel L. Clemens (Mark Twain), *Life on the Mississippi,* 1883 (N.Y: Bantam Books, 1960), 187.

21. *American Architect and Building News*, 10 May 1877.

22. It was a custom in the military to sell furniture to a successor, both to avoid freighting it and to raise funds for the trip to the next post. The practice is mentioned in most army-wife memoirs—La Tourrette's on page eight.

23. Simmons, *New Mexico*, 11.

24. Paul Horgan, "Preface to an Unwritten Book," *Yale Review* 65 (March, 1976): 321–335.

25. Horgan, "Preface," 323.

26. Paul Horgan, "Foreword" to *Main Line West* (N.Y: Harper, 1936), xii.

27. Paul Horgan, *A Distant Trumpet* (N.Y: Farrar, Straus & Giroux, 1960), 31.

28. Horgan, *A Distant Trumpet*, 97–98.

29. Horgan, *A Distant Trumpet*, 101.

30. Horgan, *A Distant Trumpet*, 250.

31. Horgan, *A Distant Trumpet*, 101.

32. Horgan, *A Distant Trumpet*, 450.

33. Horgan, *A Distant Trumpet*, 448–449.

34. Horgan, *A Distant Trumpet*, 457.

35. La Tourrette, *Fort Union Memories*, 7.

36. Horgan, "Preface," 323.

CHAPTER 4: *Town and Ranch Houses, 1880s*

1. Simmons, *New Mexico*, 159.
2. *The New Mexican*, 19 Sept. 1880.
3. *The New Mexican*, 12 Nov. 1880.
4. *The New Mexican*, 13 Nov. 1880. In error, this edition carries the date November 12 on page 2 only.
5. *The New Mexican*, 14 Dec. 1880.
6. *The New Mexican*, 24 Sept. 1880.
7. *The New Mexican*, 29 Oct. 1880.
8. *The New Mexican*, 12 Nov. 1880.
9. *The New Mexican*, 10 Dec. 1880.
10. *The New Mexican*, 14 Oct. 1880.
11. *The New Mexican*, 18 Dec. 1880.
12. *The New Mexican*, 23 June 1880.
13. Crocchiola, *Springer*, 3.
14. C. M. Chase, *The Editor's Run in New Mexico and Colorado* (Fort Davis, Tex: Frontier Press, 1968), 43.
15. In 1880, Wagon Mound was called Santa Clara. It was then called Pinkerton for a brief period before being named Wagon Mound in 1882. *Comprehensive Plan of Wagon Mound, New Mexico* (Albuquerque: Kenneth W. Larsen, 1970), 1.
16. Owen Wister, *The Virginian: A Horseman of the Plains*. 1902 (N.Y: Macmillan, 1956), 9.
17. Of course, Wister's description must be understood as tailored to illustrate one of his themes, the redeeming nature of the West. He goes on to say, in this passage about forlorn Western towns, "yet serene above their foulness swam a pure and quiet light, such as the East never sees; they might be bathing in the air of creation's first morning." Wister, *The Virginian*, 9.
18. Ralph E. Twitchell, *Leading Facts of New Mexican History*, (Cedar Rapids; Torch Press, 1911), 79–83.
19. Twitchell, *Leading Facts of New Mexican History*, 79–83.
20. Motto, *Old Houses of New Mexico*, 50.
21. Vincent J. Scully, Jr., *The Shingle Style and the Stick Style: Architectural Theory and Design from Downing to the Origins of Wright* (New Haven: Yale University, 1971), xxi.
22. *American Architect and Building News*, 3 July 1880.
23. A. J. Bicknell, Supplement to *Bicknell's Village Builder: A Victorian Architectural Guidebook*. 1872 (Watkins Glen, N.Y: American Life Foundation, 1976), plates 6–9.

24. A. J. Bicknell and William T. Comstock, *Victorian Architecture: Two Pattern Books by A.J. Bicknell and William T. Comstock* (Watkins Glen, N.Y: American Life Foundation, 1975), plates 18, 40.

25. Bainbridge Bunting, *Houses of Boston's Back Bay, An Architectural History 1840–1917* (Cambridge, Mass: Belknap Press, 1967), 281.

This feature [an elevator] was first employed in a private Back Bay house in 1876 though it had been installed in the area five years earlier in two apartment buildings. As late as 1890 the elevator was still an exceptional feature, there being in all the district only forty-four installations. Thought of at first as no substitute for stairs but as a utilitarian trunk and furniture hoist, this feature was situated in the service hall.

26. These stories were related by Mrs. Myrtle Clegg, owner of the house at the time of the interview on April 5, 1980.

27. Miguel Antonio Otero, *My Life on the Frontier, 1864–1882: Incidents and Characters of the Period When Kansas, Colorado, and New Mexico Were Passing Through the Last of their Wild and Romantic Years* (N.Y: Press of the Pioneers, 1935), 23.

28. Motto, *Old Houses of New Mexico*, 50.

29. *Raton Range*, 20 Oct. 1904.

30. Ruth W. Armstrong, *The Chases of Cimarron: Birth of the Cattle Industry in Cimarron Country: 1867–1900* (Albuquerque: New Mexico Stockman, 1981), 23.

31. Armstrong, *The Chases of Cimarron*, 59.

32. Armstrong, *The Chases of Cimarron*, 60.

33. Armstrong, *The Chases of Cimarron*, 60.

34. Gretchen Sammis, owner of the Chase ranch, in an interview October 25, 1979.

35. H.V.B., "Studies of Interior Decoration II," *American Architect and Building News*, 10 March 1877.

36. Stamped sheet metal, often in complex patterns, was used for exteriors, walls and ceilings, both in domestic and commercial installations.

37. Armstrong, *The Chases of Cimarron*, 110. An account of the Maxwell mansion may be found in Chapter Two above.

38. Armstrong, *The Chases of Cimarron*, 110.

39. Talbot Hamlin, *Greek Revival Architecture in America: Being an Account of Important Trends in American Architecture and American Life Prior to the War Between the States* (N.Y: Dover, 1944), 128.

40. Hamlin gives a number of typical plans including two parlors or drawing rooms, as on pages 134 and 305 in *Greek Revival Architecture in America*.

41. *American Architect*, 20 July 1878.

42. Mary Chase was the second Chase sister to marry Charles Springer. In 1884 he married Mary's older sister, Lottie, who died in 1893.

43. Armstrong, *The Chases of Cimarron*, 92.

44. Armstrong, *The Chases of Cimarron*, 100.

45. According to Sammis, the coal mine yielded fuel until the mid-twentieth century, when bureaucratic regulations made it impossible for the owners to allow small local operators to mine it. Interview, October 25, 1979.

46. Manville Chapman, *Raton, New Mexico*, a pamphlet issued by Raton Chamber of Commerce, 1935.

47. Chapman, *Raton, New Mexico*, 1. Chapman says a number of buildings are still (as of 1935) standing on their second foundations, but does not identify them.

48. In the more modest neighborhoods, Queen Anne style was not dominant. For example, Thomas Schwachheim arrived in Raton in 1880 to be first a miner, then a saloonkeeper. He built his adobe house in 1885 at 336 Sugarite. Heavily remodeled about the time of the First World War, it is a small, thirty-seven foot square, now peaked-roof house with a sleeping loft. According to his grandson and present owner of the house, Thomas Burch, Schwachheim planted the first orchard in northern New Mexico, covering the entire block surrounding his house.

49. J. C. Furnas, *The Americans: A Social History of the United States: 1587–1914* (N.Y: Putnam, 1969), 616.

50. Bunting, *Early Architecture*, 109.

51. Myra Ellen Jenkins, New Mexico historian, is the author of the following information which is in the New Mexico State Archives:

> Shuler was born July 23, 1858, near Grove Hills, Virginia. In 1880 he graduated from the Medical School of the University of New York City, went to Kansas for a few months, then decided to begin his practice in the new railroad town of Raton where he arrived in 1881 . . . He was Mayor of Raton for most of his life, serving in that position from 1883–1894, 1899–1902, and intermittently from 1909–1919 . . . As mayor of Raton, he was responsible for the construction of the city sanitary sewer system, jail, fire department, parks, and Carnegie Library, as well

as the Municipal Building. The house was the home of the Shuler family which included Evelyn, well-known Raton librarian. . . . The original receipts for his construction [of his house] and furnishings are in the Shuler-Berninghaus Papers of the Archives Division of the State Records Center.

Jenkins, Historical Report, March 19, 1970.
An examination of the receipts for construction indicates that Dr. Shuler was his own contractor, as there are separate receipts for monies paid to different men for foundation, carpentering, plumbing, etc.

52. The Raton Museum dates the photographs of the enlarged Shuler house as 1884, but it seems more likely that the two-story addition was built in 1896. On June 4 of that year *The Raton Range* reported that Dr. Shuler was greatly enlarging and improving his house. The reason for its being included in a discussion of houses of the 1880s rather than the probable later date of the additions is that the personality of the Shuler home was established when it was first built and was enhanced rather than changed by the enlargements.

53. Scully, *Shingle Style*, 5.

54. Scully, *Shingle Style*, 73.

55. The presence of the doll may not be good evidence as it also appears in the parlor photograph, obviously a favorite possession. The rocking chair, however, seems to be intended for more than ornament in a passageway.

CHAPTER 5 : *Adobes with Icing, 1890s*

1. Oliver La Farge, *Behind the Mountains* (Cambridge, Mass: Houghton Mifflin, 1956), 1.

2. La Farge, *Behind the Mountains*, 1–2.

3. T. M. Pearce, ed., *New Mexico Place Names: A Geographical Dictionary* (Albuquerque: University of New Mexico Press, 1965), 133.
Also, La Farge, *Behind the Mountains*, 168.

4. La Farge, *Behind the Mountains*, 3.

5. Interview with owners of Gascón Ranch, Mr. and Mrs. James E. Bartley, October 26, 1979.

6. Bartley interview, October 26, 1979.

7. Bartley interview, October 26, 1979.

8. Of course, Dunn not only had experience as a carpenter, but

he had the support of an established family of in-laws. Chase was making his own way and might understandably have had less time and money for frivolous details.

9. *Montgomery Ward & Co. Catalogue and Buyer's Guide: No. 57, Spring and Summer, 1895.* Facsimile ed. (N.Y: Dover, 1969), 389.

10. Bicknell, Supplement to *Village Builder*, 8.

11. *Montgomery Ward Catalogue*, 340.

12. *Montgomery Ward Catalogue*, 341.

13. *Sears Roebuck Catalogue: 1897.* Facsimile ed. (N.Y: Chelsea House, 1976), item numbers 9543, 9544, 9545. Pages are not numbered.

14. *Santa Fe Daily New Mexican*, 8 Oct. 1899.

15. "The Eugenie Shonnard House: 1411 Paseo de Peralta," *The Historic Santa Fe Foundation Bulletin* (November/December 1977), 2.

16. The information is from files of the Historic Santa Fe Foundation.

17. *Sears Catalogue, 1897*, items 14432–14435.

18. *Sears Catalogue, 1897*, items 14410–14419.

19. Historic Santa Fe Foundation, *Old Santa Fe Today*, rev. ed. (Albuquerque, University of New Mexico Press, 1982), 99. Research was done by State Archivist Dr. Myra Ellen Jenkins before the house was listed on city and state historical registers.

20. Alice Bullock, "Early Urban," *The New Mexican*, 8 Oct. 1972, Viva section. Article based on research cited in note 19.

21. The Historic Santa Fe Foundation is a non-profit organization devoted to the preservation of historic structures. By documenting and plaquing historic buildings it encourages owners to preserve them and, if necessary to prevent destruction or mutilation, acquires such structures.

22. An advertisement for such tiles is included in Bicknell's Supplement to the *Village Builder*.

23. The older Jaramillo house is an example of the growth of a traditional New Mexican house plan. However large, it is still a sequence of rooms in single file. In 1979 two of the original sections remained, the northern wing next to the river and the central portion.

24. Cleofas Jaramillo, *Romance of a Little Village Girl* (San Antonio, Tex: Naylor, 1955), 58.

25. "My eight rooms finished, Ven thought of adding a second story," Jaramillo, *Romance*, 13. That the second story was an afterthought is evident in the obtrusion of the second stair flight into the ceiling of the center left downstairs room.

26. Jaramillo, *Romance*, 90.

27. *Montgomery Ward Catalogue*, 384.

28. See Chapter Four for a discussion of the living hall.

29. Probably the spindle frieze with its flat-cut medallions was a purchased ornament, and side panels of plain lattice were made by the local carpenters.

30. Realistically, the Jaramillos traveled during the cold weather, and within a few years built a winter home in Santa Fe.

31. Jaramillo, *Romance*, 61.

32. Jaramillo refers to the following in *Romance*: children's party, 90; traveling troupes, 22; political meetings, 98; square dancing and dancing to the pianola, 96–97.

33. Cleofas Jaramillo inherited an urge to be in style architecturally.

My father, always keeping up with the times, took a notion to tear down the old-style porches and replace them with new white ones. The old ones had the best woodwork—thick round posts, carved lintels and scroll-cut corbels supported the round beams and the time-stained ceilings.

Jaramillo, *Romance*, 11.

34. Jaramillo, *Romance*, 96.

35. The Romólo Martínez house is traditional and very old, its construction date unknown. Built around a placita and entered through a zaguán, the house was divided between two branches of the family. The east half has a pitched roof over the original flat roof; the west half has a second story reached by an outside stair and second-story portal.

36. Jaramillo, 60.

CHAPTER 6 : *Lodge, Mansion, and Bungalow, Early 1900s*

1. The Maestes house was built by Frederico and Seleustino Maestes for their two familes. Frederico lived in the wing facing west and Seleustino in the wing facing south; each had four or five children. There was originally no fireplace and only an outside stair. The walls are 24–inch adobe. The original flat roof was changed to a peaked metal roof in 1914 when a lumber mill began operation in La Madera. At the same time some decoration was added to the porches. Information was obtained from Uvaldo Gallegos of La Madera, interview March 14, 1979.

2. This and the following information were obtained in an interview with Anne Haslanger, a summer resident of Vermejo Park and a student of its history. Interview December 5, 1978.

3. According to Haslanger, Silsbee began his career in the office of Frank Lloyd Wright.

4. Haslanger interview, December 5, 1978.

5. Haslanger interview, December 5, 1978.

6. Hugh Morrison, *Early American Architecture: From the First Colonial Settlements to the National Period* (N.Y: Oxford University Press, 1952), 73. Morrison reproduces a picture of this conjectural restoration.

7. William Pierce Randel, *The Evolution of American Taste: The History of American Style from 1607 to the Present* (N.Y: Crown, Rutledge, 1978), 102.

8. Haslanger says the tapestries had to be removed because of water damage and the tile covered by carpet because the tile was discolored during an attempt to clean it. Haslanger interview, December 5, 1978.

9. Haslanger interview, December 5, 1978.

10. Haslanger interview, December 5, 1978.

11. Haslanger interview, December 5, 1978.

12. Haslanger interview, December 5, 1978.

13. Haslanger interview, December 5, 1978.

14. Anne Haslanger, ed., *A History of Vermejo Park* (Vermejo Park, n.d.), 6–8.

15. As of 1982, the gifts did not include any buildings.

16. On November 28, 1905, Alva Hobbs ran an advertisement in the *Raton Daily Range* which listed twenty-five carloads of hardware goods and read in part:

Hobbs Hardware Company was organized August 29th, 1905, at the request of many leading property owners and business men of this section and for the purpose of both providing an establishment where all kinds of merchandise pertaining to a general line of HARDWARE, STEAM FITTING, HEATING and PLUMBING, could be bought in any quantity needed at prices which would justify both the large and small buyer in patronizing the institution and not be forced to send out of the City and Territory for anything needed in above lines, and ALSO FOR THE PURPOSE OF MAKING MONEY, which we hope to do. [The capitalization is original.] On the Rapp and Rapp firm see Carl D. Sheppard, *Creator of the Santa Fe Style: Isaac Hamilton Rapp, Architect* (Albuquerque: University of New Mexico Press, 1988).

17. *American Architect*, 13 Aug. 1881, 72–73.

18. *American Architect*, 13 Aug. 1881, 73.

19. William Nelson Black, "Various Causes for Bad Architecture," *The Architectural Record*, (October–December, 1892), 156.

20. Black, *Architectural Record*, 156.

21. Black, *Architectural Record*, 156.

22. *American Architect*, 15 Sept. 1900.

23. Randel, *Evolution of American Taste*, 145.

24. Randel, *Evolution of American Taste*, 142.

25. "Arts and Crafts Movement," *The Britannica Encyclopedia of American Art* (Chicago: Encyclopaedia Britannica Educational Corporation, n.d.), 48.

26. Marshall B. Davidson, *The American Heritage History of Notable American Houses* (N.Y: American Heritage, 1971), 306.

27. According to David Gebhard, architectural historian, "Shingle Style" is "a term popularized in the early 1950s by the architectural historian Vincent Scully." *Encyclopedia of American Art*, 507.

28. Frank Lloyd Wright, *The Natural House* (N.Y: Bramhall House, 1954), 14.

29. Gebhard, "Greene, Charles S. (1868–1957) and Henry M. (1870–1954)," *Encyclopedia of American Art*, 248.

30. Randel, *Evolution of American Taste*, 145.

31. This information is contained in a report on the house filed with the New Mexico State Archives in Santa Fe when the house was nominated for a plaque by the Cultural Properties Review Committee. The signature on the report appears to be "J. Iowa."

CHAPTER 7 : *Enduring Adobe*

1. Simmons, *New Mexico*, 18.

2. Ibid. Fray Marcos, seeking the legendary Seven Cities of Cibola and suffering from the murder of his companions and fear of venturing farther, saw the pueblo of Hawikuh from a distant hill.

3. Charles F. Lummis, *The Land of Poco Tiempo*. 1893 (N.Y: Scribner's, 1928), 1–2.

4. Mabel Dodge Lujan, "Paso por Aqui!" *New Mexico Quarterly*, (Summer, 1951), 140.

5. The Spanish-Pueblo Revival might be said to have been initiated by the 1909 remodeling of Hodgin Hall on the University of New Mexico Campus from Richardson Romanesque to Santa Fe Style. The Revival's biggest impetus came from the New Mexico building at the 1915 Panama-California Exposition in San Diego and the building it inspired, the 1916 Museum of Fine Arts in Santa Fe.

6. Sylvanus Griswold Morley, "Santa Fe Architecture." *Old Santa Fe*, (January, 1915): 279–301.

7. Josiah Gregg, *Commerce of the Prairies*, xxvii.

8. Rexford Newcomb, *Spanish Colonial Architecture in the United States*, 29.

Glossary

Definitions marked* are adapted from Henry H. Saylor, *Dictionary of Architecture* (N.Y: John Wiley and Sons, 1952).

Acequia   An irrigation ditch.

Baluster*   A miniature column or other upright which, in series, supports a handrail.

Balustrade*   A railing consisting of a handrail on balusters or columns.

Batter*   A slope upward and backward from the perpendicular in a wall or pier.

Banco   In New Mexico, a built-in bench of the wall material, usually adobe.

Beehive   In New Mexico, a fireplace built into a corner, oval-shaped like a beehive with an elliptical opening.

Capital*   In architecture, the top member or group of members of a column.

Casement*   A window, the sash or sashes of which are hinged on the jamb (side).

Corbel   A bracket of building material such as wood, stone, or brick, projecting from the wall for the purpose of supporting a ceiling beam.

Cornice*   A decorative development of the coping edging the eaves of a roof.

Facade   An exterior face of a building.

Fanega   A measure of wheat equaling about two bushels.

Fenestration*   The disposition of windows in a facade.

Four-light, six-light, etc.   A light is a pane of glass, thus four-pane, six-pane, etc.

Gable   The triangle formed at the end of a pitched roof, also the term gabled referring to a roof which forms these triangles.

Jacal   A method of construction involving vertical wood posts set in the ground; the spaces between are filled with mud.

Latias   Peeled aspen or cottonwood poles laid diagonally or at right angles across vigas or beams to form a ceiling.

Lintel   The horizontal beam across the top of a window or door frame.

Mansard roof*   A roof having a slope in two planes, the lower plane usually being much steeper than the higher plane.

Parapet*   A low retaining wall at the edge of a roof.

Pediment   The triangular face of a roof gable, or this triangular shape reflected in the upper horizontal member of a window or door facing.

Pilaster   A supporting column or pillar with a capital and base, set partially into a wall as an ornamental motif.

Placita   In New Mexico, a courtyard encircled by the wings of a house or by several houses.

Portal   In New Mexico, a porch that is open but covered by a roof.

Puddled adobe   Southwest Indian method of construction, involving successive layers of hand-shaped mud, each course drying before the next is applied.

Ricos   In New Mexico, persons of wealth.

Sala   A reception or drawing room.

Terrones   Blocks cut from sod with roots left intact for bonding.

Vara   Measure of about 33 inches, varying from 32–43 inches.

Viga   A log with the bark peeled off, used as a ceiling beam.

Zaguán   Covered passage into a courtyard.

Selected Sources

I. Books, Articles, and Unpublished Papers

Abert, J. W. *Western America in 1846–47: The Original Travel Diary of Lieutenant J. W. Abert Who Mapped New Mexico for the United States Army: With Illustrations in Color from his Sketchbook.* Edited by John Galvin. San Francisco: John Howell Books, 1966.

Andrews, Wayne. *Architecture in America: A Photographic History from the Colonial Period to the Present.* New York: Atheneum, 1960.

———. *Architecture in Chicago and Mid America: A Photographic History.* New York: Atheneum, 1968.

Armstrong, Ruth W. *The Chases of Cimarron: Birth of the Cattle Industry in Cimarron Country: 1867–1900.* Albuquerque: New Mexico Stockman, 1981.

Austin, Mary. *Earth Horizon: Autobiography.* New York: Literary Guild, 1932.

———. *The Land of Little Rain.* Garden City, N.Y: Doubleday, Anchor Books, 1902.

Bailey, Jessie Bromilow. *Diego de Vargas and the Reconquest of New Mexico.* Albuquerque: University of New Mexico Press, 1940.

Bancroft, Hubert Howe. *History of Arizona and New Mexico: 1530–1888.* Vol. 17, *The Works of Hubert Howe Bancroft.* New York: McGraw–Hill, 1889.

Bandelier, Adolf F. *The Delight Makers.* New York: Dodd, Mead, 1890–1916.

Beck, Warren A. and Ynez D. Haase. *Historical Atlas of New Mexico.* Norman: University of Oklahoma Press, 1969.

Bell, William A. *New Tracks in North America: A Journal of Travel and Adventure Whilst Engaged in the Survey for a Southern Railroad to the Pacific Ocean During 1867–8.* 1870. Reprint. Albuquerque: Horn & Wallace, 1965.

Bemier, Georges and Rosamond, eds. *The Best in Twentieth Century Architecture.* New York: Bemier, n.d.

Bicknell, A.J. and William T. Comstock. *Victorian Architecture: Two Pattern Books by A.J. Bicknell and William T. Comstock.* Watkins Glen, N.Y: American Life Foundation, 1975.

Bicknell, A. J. *Village Builder: A Victorian Architectural Guidebook.* 1872. Watkins Glen, N.Y: American Life Foundation, 1976.

Biebel, Charles D. "Cultural Change on the Southwest Frontier: Albuquerque Schooling, 1870–1895." *New Mexico Historical Review* 55:3 (September, 1980): 208–230.

Black, William Nelson. "Various Causes for Bad Architecture." *The Architectural Record,* October/December, 1892:149–164.

Blumenson, John. *Identifying American Architecture.* Nashville: American Association for State and Local History, 1977.

Boorstin, Daniel J. *The Americans: The Democratic Experience.* New York: Random House, 1973.

Boyd, E. *Popular Arts of Spanish New Mexico.* Santa Fe: Museum of New Mexico Press, 1974.

Britannica Encyclopedia of American Art. Chicago: Encyclopaedia Britannica Educational Corporation, n.d..

Bradford, Richard. *Red Sky at Morning.* New York: Pocket Books, 1968.

———. *So Far From Heaven.* Philadelphia: Lippincott, 1973.

Brayer, Garnet M. ed. *Land of Enchantment: Memoirs of Marian Russell Along the Santa Fe Trail: as Dictated to Mrs. Hal Russell.* Evanston: Branding Iron, 1954.

Bryant, Keith L. Jr. *History of the Atchison, Topeka and Santa Fe Railway.* New York: Macmillan, 1974.

Bullock, Alice. *Mountain Villages.* Rev. ed. Santa Fe: Sunstone, 1981.

———. "Watrous: A Living Relic Where Rivers Meet." *The New Mexican.* Undated clipping in New Mexico State Archives.

Bunting, Bainbridge. "An Architectural Guide to Northern New Mexico." *New Mexico Architecture* 12, nos. 9/10 (September/October 1970): 13–50.

———. *Early Architecture in New Mexico.* Albuquerque: University of New Mexico Press, 1976.

———. *Houses of Boston's Back Bay: An Architectural History 1840–1917.* Cambridge, Mass: Belknap Press, 1967.

———. *Taos Adobes: Spanish Colonial and Territorial Architecture of the Taos Valley*. Santa Fe: Museum of New Mexico Press, 1964.

Calhoun, James S. *The Official Correspondence of James S. Calhoun*, ed. Annie Heloise Able. Washington, D.C: U. S. Government Printing Office, 1915.

Campa, Arthur L. *Hispanic Culture in the Southwest*. Norman: University of Oklahoma Press, 1979.

Caperton, Thomas J. *Rogue! Being an Account of the Life and High Times of Stephen W. Dorsey, United States Senator and New Mexico Cattle Baron . . . now Accessible to the Public!!!* Santa Fe: Museum of New Mexico Press, 1978.

Chapman, Manville. *Raton, New Mexico*, a pamphlet issued by Raton Chamber of Commerce, 1935.

Chase, C.M. *The Editor's Run in New Mexico and Colorado*. Fort Davis, Texas: Frontier Press, 1968.

Cleaveland, Agnes Morley. *No Life for a Lady*. Boston: Houghton Mifflin, 1941.

———. *Satan's Paradise: From Lucien Maxwell to Fred Lambert*. Boston: Houghton Mifflin, 1952.

Cleaveland, Norman, with George Fitzpatrick. *The Morleys: Young Upstarts on the Southwest Frontier*. Albuquerque: Calvin Horn, 1971.

Clemens, Samuel L. (Mark Twain). *Life on the Mississippi*. 1883. New York: Bantam Books, 1960.

Conron, John. "Old and New Architecture . . . Design Relationships." *New Mexico Architecture* 20:3 (May/June 1978): 10–14.

———. *Socorro: A Historic Survey*. University of New Mexico Press, 1980.

Connor, Seymour V. and Jimmy M. Skaggs. *Broadcloth and Britches: The Santa Fe Trade*. College Station: Texas A & M Press, 1977.

Cooper, H.J. *The Art of Furnishing: On Rational and Aesthetic Principles*. New York: Henry Holt, 1881.

Crocchiola, F. Stanley. *The Springer, New Mexico, Story*. Pantex, Texas: n.p., 1962.

———. *The Watrous, New Mexico, Story*. Pantex, Texas: n.p., 1962.

Cummings, Marcus Fayette and Charles Crosby Miller. *Victorian Architectural Details: Two Pattern Books by Marcus Fayette Cummings and Charles Crosby Miller*. 1868, 1873; Watkins Glen, New York: American Life Foundation, 1978.

Curry, George. *George Curry: 1861–1947: An Autobiography*. Edited by H. B. Hening. Albuquerque: University of New Mexico Press, 1958.

Davidson, Marshall B. *The American Heritage History of Notable American Houses.* New York: American Heritage, 1971.

Davis, W.W.H. *El Gringo: or New Mexico and Her People.* Santa Fe: Rydal Press, 1938.

Design and Preservation in Santa Fe: A Pluralistic Approach. Santa Fe: Santa Fe City Planning Dept., 1977.

Dickey, Roland F. *New Mexico Village Arts.* Albuquerque: University of New Mexico Press, 1970.

Downing, Andrew Jackson. *The Architecture of Country Houses.* Reprint. New York: DaCap, 1968.

Downing, Antoinette F. and Vincent J. Scully. *The Architectural Heritage of Newport, Rhode Island: 1640–1915.* Cambridge, Mass: Harvard University Press, 1952.

Emmet, Boris, and John E. Jeuck. *Catalogues and Counters: A History of Sears, Roebuck & Co.* Chicago: University of Chicago Press, 1950.

Estergreen, M. Morgan. *Kit Carson: A Portrait in Courage.* Norman: University of Oklahoma Press, 1962.

Fergusson, Erna. *New Mexico: A Pageant of Three Peoples.* New York: Alfred A. Knopf, 1966.

Fergusson, Harvey. *Grant of Kingdom.* 1950. Paperback ed., Albuquerque: University of New Mexico, Zia Books, 1975.

———. *Home in the West: An Inquiry into My Origins.* New York: Duell, Sloan and Pearce, 1944.

Field, Matt. *Matt Field on the Santa Fe Trail.* Collected by Clyde and Mae Reed Porter. Edited by John E. Sunder. Norman: University of Oklahoma Press, 1960.

Furnas, J.C. *The Americans: A Social History of the United States: 1587–1914.* New York: Putnam, 1969.

Garrard, Lewis H. *Wah-to-Yah and the Taos Trail.* Vol. 4, Southwest Historical Series. Edited by Ralph P. Bieber. Glendale, California: Arthur H. Clark, 1938.

Gebhard, David. "Architecture and the Fred Harvey Houses." *New Mexico Architecture* 4:7/8 (July/August 1962): 11–18, and 6, nos. 1/2 (January/February 1964): 18–25.

Gibbs, James. *A Book of Architecture Containing Designs of Buildings and Ornaments.* London: 1728. Reprint. New York: Benjamin Blom, 1968.

Girouard, Mark. *Life in the English Country House: A Social and Architectural History.* New Haven: Yale University Press, 1978.

Gowans, Alan. *Images of American Living: Four Centuries of Architecture and Furniture as Cultural Expression.* New York: Harper & Row, 1964.

Grant, Blanche C. *When Old Trails Were New: The Story of Taos.* Chicago: Rio Grande Press, 1963.

Gregg, Andrew K. *New Mexico in the Nineteenth Century: A Pictorial History.* Albuquerque: University of New Mexico Press, 1968.

Gregg, Josiah. *Commerce of the Prairies: The Journal of a Santa Fe Trader.* 1844. Reprint. Dallas: Southwest Press, 1933.

Gritzner, Charles. "Hispanic Log Construction of New Mexico." *El Palacio* 85:4 (Winter, 1979–80).

Grove, Pearce S. et al. *New Mexico Newspapers: A Comprehensive Guide to Bibliographic Entries and Locations.* Albuquerque: University of New Mexico Press, 1975.

Hamlin, Talbot Faulkner. *The American Spirit in Architecture.* Vol. 13, *The Pageant of America: A Pictorial History of the United States.* Edited by Ralph Henry Gabriel. New Haven: Yale University Press, 1926.

———. *Greek Revival Architecture in America: Being an Account of Important Trends in American Architecture and American Life Prior to the War Between the States.* New York: Dover, 1944.

Hammond, George P. *The Adventures of Alexander Barclay: Mountain Man.* Denver: Old West, 1976.

Handlin, David P. *The American Home: Architecture and Society*: 1815–1915. Boston: Little, Brown, 1979.

Harvey, Clara Toombs. *Not So Wild the Old West: A Collection of Facts, Fables and Fun.* Denver: Golden Bell Press, 1961.

Haslanger, Anne, ed., *A History of Vermejo Park.* Vermejo Park, n.d.

Hewett, Edgar Lee. *Man and Culture.* Vol. 3, *Man in the Pageant of the Ages.* Albuquerque: University of New Mexico, 1944.

Hindle, Brooke. "How Much is a Piece of the True Cross Worth." *Material Culture and the Study of American Life.* Edited by Ian M.G. Quimby. New York: W.W. Norton, 1978.

Historic Preservation Program for New Mexico: Vol. 2, The Inventory. Santa Fe: State Planning Office, 1973.

Historic Santa Fe Foundation Bulletin 3:3 (November/December 1977): 1–6.

Historic Santa Fe Foundation. *Old Santa Fe Today.* Rev. ed. Albuquerque: University of New Mexico Press, 1982.

Holly, Henry Hudson. *Modern Dwellings in Town and Country Adapted to American Wants and Climate.* New York: n.p., 1878.

Horgan, Paul. *The Centuries of Santa Fe.* New York: Dutton, 1956.

———. *A Distant Trumpet.* New York: Farrar, Straus & Giroux, 1960.

———. "Foreword" to *Main Line West.* New York: Harper, 1936.

———. *Josiah Gregg and His Vision of the Early West.* New York: Farrar, Straus & Giroux, 1972.

———. "Preface to an Unwritten Book," *Yale Review* 65 (March, 1976): 321–335.

Howells, William Dean. *Hazard of New Fortunes*. New York: Boni and Liveright, 1889.

———. *The Rise of Silas Lapham*. 1885. New York: Rinehart, 1949.

Hume, Ivor Noel. "Material Culture with the Dirt on It: A Virginia Perspective." *Material Culture and the Study of American Life.* Edited by Ian M.G. Quimby. New York: W.W. Norton, 1978:33.

Inman, Colonel Henry. *The Old Santa Fe Trail: The Story of a Great Highway*. 1898. Topeka, Kansas: Crane, 1916.

Isham, Norman Morrison. *Early American Houses and a Glossary of Colonial Architectural Terms*. New York: Da Capo, 1967.

Ivers, Louise Harris. "The Architecture of Las Vegas, New Mexico." Dissertation, University of New Mexico, 1975.

———. "La Cueva." Master's Thesis, New Mexico Highlands University, 1972.

Jackson, Donald, ed. *The Journals of Zebulon Montgomery Pike*, 2 vols. Norman: University of Oklahoma Press, 1966.

Jaramillo, Cleofas. *Romance of a Little Village Girl*. San Antonio, Texas: Naylor, 1955.

———. *Shadows of the Past*. Santa Fe: Ancient City Press, 1972.

Jenkins, Myra Ellen, and Albert Schroeder. *A Brief History of New Mexico*. Albuquerque: University of New Mexico Press, 1974.

Johnson, William Templeton. "The Santa Fe of the Future." No. 39, *Papers of the School of American Archaeology*. Santa Fe: 1916.

Jones, Billy M. *Health-Seekers in the Southwest, 1817–1900*. Norman: University of Oklahoma Press, 1967.

Keleher, William A. *Maxwell Land Grant: A New Mexico Item*. Santa Fe: Rydal, 1942.

Kidney, Walter C. *The Architecture of Choice: Eclecticism in America, 1880–1930*. New York: George Braziller, 1974.

Koeper, Frederick. *Illinois Architecture: From Territorial Times to the Present: A Selective Guide*. Chicago: University of Chicago Press, 1968.

Kronenberger, Louis, ed. *Quality: Its Image in the Arts*. New York: Atheneum, 1969.

Kubler, George. *The Religious Architecture of New Mexico: In the Colonial Period and Since the American Occupation.* 1940. Reprint. Albuquerque: University of New Mexico Press, 1972.

Lacy, James M. "New Mexican Women in Early American Writing." *New Mexico Historical Review* 34:1 (Spring, 1964): 41–51.

La Farge, Oliver. *Behind the Mountains*. Cambridge, Mass: Houghton Mifflin, 1956.

————. *Santa Fe: Autobiography of a Southwestern Town.* Norman: University of Oklahoma Press, 1959.

Lamar, Howard Roberts. *The Far Southwest 1846–1912: A Territorial History.* New Haven: Yale University Press, 1966.

Lane, Lydia Spencer. *I Married a Soldier or Old Days in the Old Army.* 1893. Albuquerque: Horn & Wallace, 1964.

Larson, Kenneth W. and Assoc., City Planning Consultants. *Comprehensive Plan: Wagon Mound, New Mexico: New Mexico Project P–66.* Albuquerque, 1970.

La Tourrette, Genevieve. "Fort Union Memories." *New Mexico Historical Review* 26:4 (October, 1956): 277–286.

Lummis, Charles F. *The Land of Poco Tiempo.* 1893. New York: Scribner's, 1928.

Lumpkins, William. *Modern Spanish-Pueblo Homes.* Santa Fe: n.p., 1946.

Lynes, Russell. *The Domesticated Americans.* New York: Harper & Row, 1963.

————. *The Tastemakers.* New York: Harper's, 1949.

Maas, John. *The Gingerbread Age.* New York: Bramhall House, 1957.

Magoffin, Susan Shelby. *Down the Santa Fe Trail and Into Mexico: The Diary of Susan Shelby Magoffin 1846–47.* Edited by Stella M. Drumm. New Haven: Yale University Press, 1926, rev. ed., 1962.

McKenney's Business Directory of the Principal Towns of Central and Southern California, Arizona, New Mexico, Southern Colorado and Kansas, etc. etc. Oakland, Cal., and Santa Fe: Pacific Press, 1882–83.

Minge, Ward Alan. "The Last Will and Testament of Don Severino Martínez." *New Mexico Quarterly* 33:1 (Spring, 1963):33–56.

Montgomery Ward & Co. Catalogue and Buyer's Guide: No. 57, Spring and Summer. 1895. Facsimile ed. New York: Dover, 1969.

Morley, Sylvanus. "Santa Fe Architecture. "*Old Santa Fe* 2:3 (January, 1915): 278–301.

Morrison, Hugh. *Early American Architecture: From the First Colonial Settlements to the National Period.* New York: Oxford University Press, 1952.

Motto, Sytha. *Old Houses of New Mexico and the People Who Built Them.* Albuquerque: Calvin Horn, 1972.

Mumford, Lewis. *The Brown Decades: A Study of the Arts in America 1865–1895.* New York: Dover, 1931.

Murphy, Lawrence R. "Master of the Cimarron: Lucien B. Maxwell." *New Mexico Historical Review* 55:1 (January, 1980): 5–23.

————. *Out in God's Country: A History of Colfax County, New Mex-*

ico. Springer, NM: Springer Publishing Co., 1969.

Myres, Sandra L. "Mexican Americans and Westering Anglos: A Feminine Perspective." *New Mexico Historical Review,* 57:4 (October, 1982): 317–333.

Myrick, David F. *New Mexico Railroads: An Historical Survey.* Golden, Colorado: Colorado Railroad Museum, 1970.

Newcomb, Rexford. *Spanish Colonial Architecture in the United States.* New York: J.J. Augustin, 1937.

O'Rourke, Frank. *The Far Mountains.* New York: William Morrow, 1959.

Otero, Miguel Antonio. *My Life on the Frontier 1864–1882: Incidents and Characters of the Period When Kansas, Colorado, and New Mexico were Passing Through the Last of their Wild and Romantic Years.* New York: Press of the Pioneers, 1935.

———. *My Life on the Frontier 1882–1897.* Albuquerque: University of New Mexico Press, 1939.

Parish, William J. *The Charles Ilfeld Company: A Study of the Rise and Decline of Mercantile Capitalism in New Mexico.* Cambridge, Mass: Harvard University Press, 1961.

Pearce, T.M., ed. *New Mexico Place Names: A Geographical Dictionary.* Albuquerque: University of New Mexico Press, 1965.

Pearson, Jim Berry. *The Maxwell Land Grant.* Norman: University of Oklahoma Press, 1961.

Perrigo, Lynn I. *Our Spanish Southwest.* Dallas: Banks Upshaw, 1960.

Persons, Stow. *The Decline of American Gentility.* New York: Columbia University Press, 1973.

Peterson, Harold L. *Americans at Home: From the Colonists to the Late Victorians: A Pictorial Source Book of American Domestic Interiors with an Appendix on Inns and Taverns.* New York: Scribner's, 1971.

Phipps, Frances. *Colonial Kitchens, Their Furnishings, and Their Gardens: The First Definitive Account Based on Settlers' Journals and Travelers' Diaries.* New York: Hawthorn, 1972.

Pillsbury, Dorothy L. *Adobe Doorways.* Albuquerque: University of New Mexico Press, 1952.

Platt, Frederic. *America's Gilded Age: Its Architecture and Decoration.* New York: A.S. Barnes, 1946.

Poe, Sophie A. *Buckboard Days: The Thrilling Experiences on our Southwestern Frontier of John William Poe as Buffalo Hunter, United States Marshall, Sheriff, Rancher, Banker.* Caldwell, Idaho: Caxton, 1936.

Polk's New Mexico and Arizona Pictorial State Gazetteer and Busi-

ness Directory: First Statehood Edition: 1912–1913. St.Paul: R.L. Polk & Co., 1912.

Pratt, Richard. *The Second Treasury of Early American Homes.* In collaboration with Dorothy Pratt. New York: Hawthorn, 1954.

Quimby, M.G., ed. *Material Culture and the Study of American Life.* New York: W.W. Norton, 1978.

Rak, Mary Kidder. *A Cowman's Wife.* Boston: Houghton Mifflin, 1934.

Randel, William Pierce. *The Evolution of American Taste: The History of American Style from 1607 to the Present.* New York: Crown, Rutledge, 1978.

Ritch, William G. *Illustrated New Mexico.* 5th ed. Santa Fe: Bureau of Immigration, 1885.

———. *New Mexico Blue Book, 1882.* Reprint. Albuquerque: University of New Mexico Press, 1968.

Robinson, Willard B. *American Forts: Architectural Form & Function.* 1977. Ann Arbor, Mich: University Microfilm International, Books on Demand.

———. "Colonial Ranch Architecture." *Southwestern Historical Quarterly* 83:2 (October, 1979): 123–150.

Rudisill, Richard. *Photographers of the New Mexico Territory, 1854–1912.* Santa Fe: Museum of New Mexico Press, 1973.

Rudofsky, Bernard. *Architecture Without Architects.* Garden City, N.Y: Doubleday, 1964.

Sanford, Trent Elwood. *The Architecture of the Southwest: Indian, Spanish, American.* New York: W.W. Norton, 1950.

Saylor, Henry H. *Dictionary of Architecture.* New York: John Wiley & Sons, 1952.

Schmitt, Martin F. and Dee Brown. *The Settler's West.* New York: Scribner's, 1955.

Scully, Penrose, with Prescott C. Fuller. *From Pedlars to Merchant Princes.* Chicago: Follert, 1967.

Scully, Vincent J., Jr. *The Shingle Style and the Stick Style: Architectural Theory and Design from Downing to the Origins of Wright.* New Haven: Yale University Press, 1971.

Sears Roebuck Catalogue; 1897. Facsimile reprint. New York: Chelsea House, 1976.

Segale, Sister Blandina. *At the End of the Santa Fe Trail.* Milwaukee: Bruce, 1948.

Shurtleff, Harold R. *The Log Cabin Myth: A Study of the Early Dwellings of the English Colonists in North America.* Edited and with introduction by Samuel Eliot Morrison. Cambridge, Mass: Harvard University Press, 1939.

Simmons, Marc. *New Mexico: A Bicentennial History*. New York: W.W. Norton, 1977.

Smith, Henry Nash. *Virgin Land: The American West as Symbol and Myth*. Cambridge, Mass: Harvard University Press, 1950.

Smith, G. E. Kidder. *A Pictorial History of Architecture in America*. 2 vols. New York: American Heritage, 1976.

Stallard, Patricia Y. *Glittering Misery: Dependents of the Indian Fighting Army*. San Rafael, Cal: Presidio, 1978.

Steele, James W. *Frontier Army Sketches*. 1883. Albuquerque: University of New Mexico Press, 1969.

Stocking, Hobart E. *The Road to Santa Fe*. New York: Hastings, 1971.

Stoehr, C. Eric. *Bonanza Victorian*. Albuquerque: University of New Mexico Press, 1975.

Swadesh, Frances Leon. *Los Primeros Pobladores: Hispanic Americans of the Ute Frontier*. Notre Dame: University of Notre Dame Press, 1974.

Tressman, Ruth. "Home on the Range." *New Mexico Historical Review* 26:1 (January, 1956): 1–17.

Trollope, Mrs. Frances. *Domestic Manners of the Americans*. 1832. Edited by Richard D. Heffner. New York: New American Library, 1956.

Twitchell, Ralph Emerson. *Leading Facts of New Mexican History*. 5 vols. Cedar Rapids: Torch Press, 1911.

———. *Old Santa Fe*. Santa Fe: New Mexican Publishing Co., 1925.

Utley, Robert M. *Fort Union National Monument, New Mexico*. No. 35, National Park Service Historical Handbook Series. Washington: National Park Service, 1962.

Webb, James Josiah. *Adventures in the Santa Fe Trade 1844–1847*. Vol. 1, The Southwest Historical Series. Edited by Ralph P. Bieber. Glendale, Cal: Arthur H. Clark, 1931.

Weigle, Marta. *Hispanic Villages of Northern New Mexico*. 1935: Tewa Basin Study. Reprint. Boulder: Lightning Tree, 1975.

Westphall, Victor. *Thomas Benton Catron and His Era*. Tucson: University of Arizona Press, 1973.

Wister, Owen. *The Virginian: A Horseman of the Plains*. 1902; New York: Macmillan, Pocketbooks, 1956.

Wilson, H.T. *Historical Sketch of Las Vegas, New Mexico*. Chicago: Hotel World, 1880.

Wooten, Mattie Lloyd, ed. *Women Tell the Story of the Southwest*. San Antonio, Tex: Naylor, 1940.

Wright, Frank Lloyd. *An American Architecture: Frank Lloyd Wright*. Edited by Edgar Kaufmann. New York: Horizon, 1955.

———. *The Natural House*. New York: Bramhall House, 1954.

II. PERIODICALS.

American Architect and Building News. 1876–1909
Architectural Record. 1891–1912
Cimarron News and Press. 1875–1881
Daily New Mexican, 1869–77, 1880–97, 1904, 1908.
Daily Optic. Las Vegas, 1879–1905.
New Mexico Architecture, 1962–82.
New Mexico Historical Review. 1956–1982.
Raton Daily Range. 1887–1908.
Santa Fe Daily New Mexican. 1899.
The New Mexican. 1972.
Weekly New Mexican. 1878–1880

III. GOVERNMENT PUBLICATIONS

Historic American Buildings Survey

Sources of Illustrations

Photographs not otherwise credited are by the author.

Abert, J. W. *Western America in 1846–47.* Fig. 1, Santa Fe; Fig. 5, Gallegos.

American Architect & Building News. Fig. 28, Roofing; Figs. 41, 74, Living Halls; Fig. 76, Plan.

Bicknell, A. J. *Village Builder: A Victorian Architectural Guidebook.* Figs. 48, 50.

Bunting, Bainbridge. *Early Architecture in New Mexico.* Fig. 7, Martínez; Fig. 12, Plan.

———. *Taos Adobes.* Figs. 15–18, Martínez.

——— Collection, University of New Mexico. Fig. 73, Shuler plan.

Cummings, Marcus Fayette, and Charles Crosby Miller, *Victorian Architectural Details.* Fig. 10.

Gregg, Andrew K. *New Mexico in the Nineteenth Century: A Pictorial History.* Fig. 2, Las Vegas; Fig. 3, Taos.

Greene & Greene Museum, Pasadena. Fig. 117, Blacker.

Historic American Buildings Survey. Figs. 30, 31, 32, Watrous; Fig. 52, Mills; Fig. 109, Morse–Libby.

Historic Santa Fe Foundation. Fig. 90, Tully.

Holly, Henry Hudson. *Modern Dwellings in Town and Country Adapted to American Wants and Climate.* Fig. 47, Hall.

Museum of New Mexico. Fig. 19, Maxwell, Neg. #7720; Fig. 20, Maxwell, Neg. #14621; Fig. 22, Cimarron, Neg. #8959; Fig. 25, Watrous, Neg. # 11685; Figs. 8, 34, 35, Ft. Union, Negs. #38218, #12849, #38174; Fig. 68, Las Vegas, Neg. #70714; Fig. 96, Jaramillo, Neg. #9934; Figs. 106, 108, 110, 112, Vermejo, Negs. #30546, #71265, #71255, #71260, by Thomas Fitzsimmons;

Figs. 119, 123, 124, Dorman, Negs. #61493, #61494, #10469, by Jesse L. Nusbaum.

National Park Service. Figs. 36, 37, 38, 39, 40, Ft. Union.

Owners' Collection. Figs. 26, 27, 29, 32, Watrous.

Owners' Collection. Figs. 55, 56, 60, 63, Chase.

Raton Museum. Figs. 69, 70, 72, 75, 77, Shuler.

Smith, G. E. Kidder. *A Pictorial History of Architecture in America.* Fig. 21, Menard.

Index